AF587718

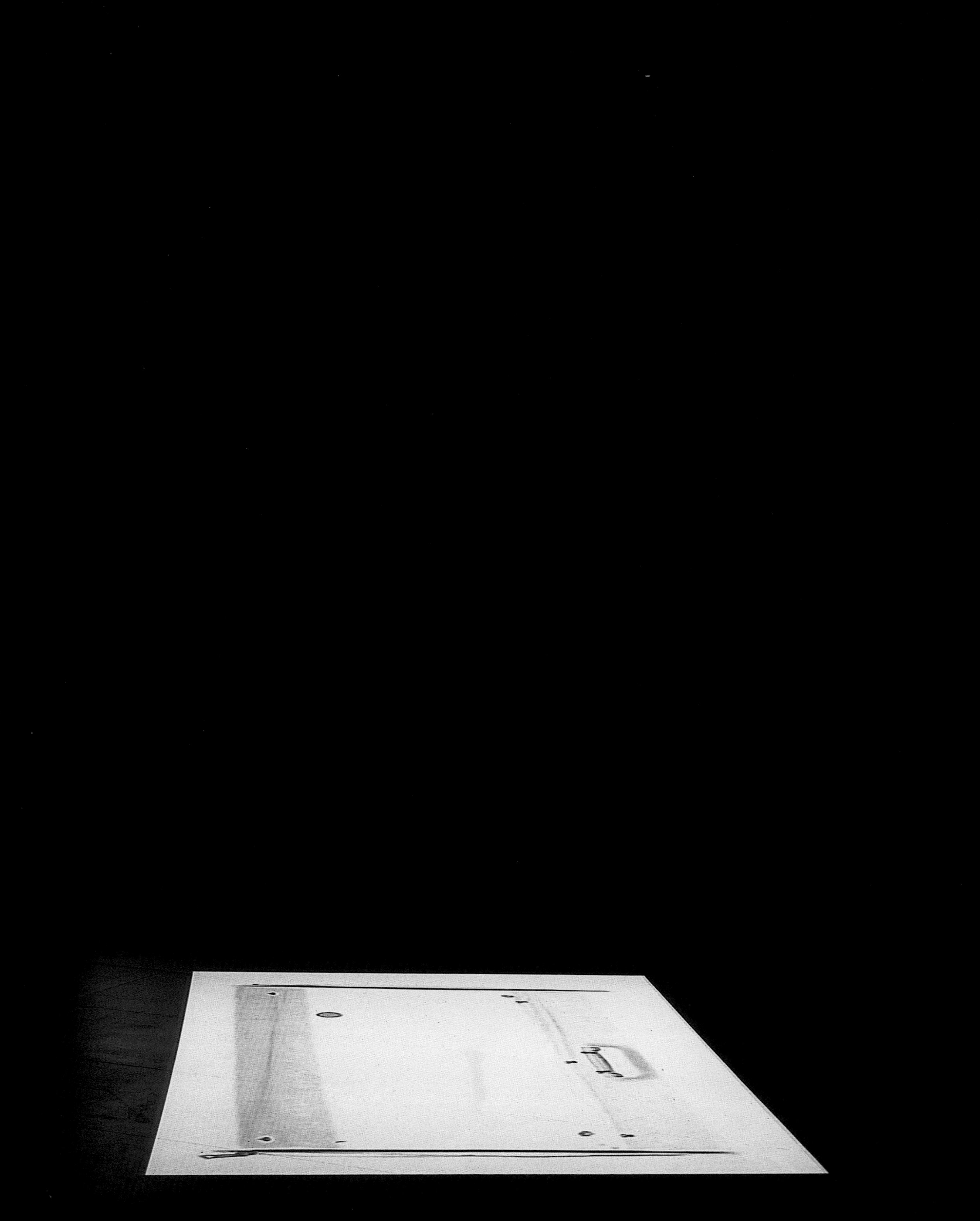

Ergin Çavuşoğlu
Places of Departure

Film and Video Umbrella
Haunch of Venison

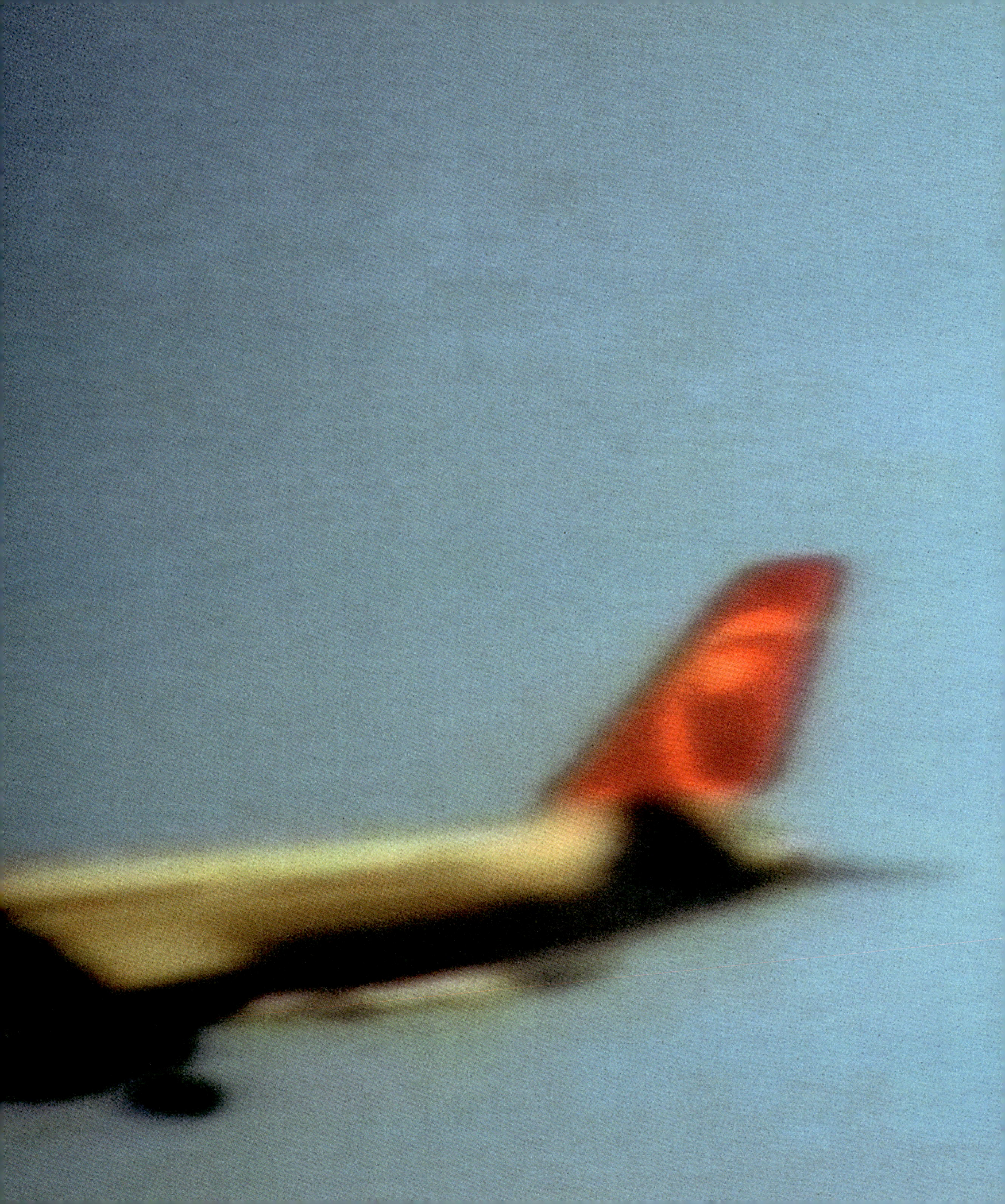

Places of Departure
Steven Bode

According to the theory of plate tectonics, the earth below us is constantly in motion. Like lilies on a pond, the continents are drifting, slowly but surely shifting position, to an extent that is virtually imperceptible within the course of a human lifespan but which will be profound and utterly transforming over a larger measure of time. Nothing is fixed, nothing is stable — not even the ground beneath our feet. If this is a slightly disconcerting thought, it is one that finds an increasing echo in our experience of modernity, in which the accelerating movement of people (and capital) from place to place and from country to country has become a defining feature of the contemporary zeitgeist. Amidst the aftershocks precipitated by some of these underlying structural changes, millions of people are having to learn to situate themselves within a new set of cultural co-ordinates. Here, too, the balance of the continents is shifting — and this time at a much more conspicuous, and remarkable, pace.

The video installations of Ergin Çavuşoğlu offer a prime view of this complex and changing landscape. Often predicated on the idea of a journey, on which we learn to travel expectantly rather than ever arrive, they deftly evoke this state of flux and this ongoing process of transition. Although much of their stamp of authenticity would appear to be drawn from the artist's own personal history of migration (born in Bulgaria as part of the minority Turkish community, Çavuşoğlu left, with his parents, for Istanbul, and now lives in London), his pieces convey something equally universal: a frisson of excitement and a murmur of dislocation that are integral to both the texture and the rhythm of contemporary experience. Stretched across multiple projection screens to better capture the multi-faceted character of modern reality, and often filmed among the crowded hubbub of places like airports or markets, Çavuşoğlu's installations also possess a heightened lyric quality that traces the arc of individual stories against the backdrop of wider social and cultural forces.

Beneath their patterns of surface complexity, Çavuşoğlu's pieces frequently reach back to older, embedded histories, as if the steady, inexorable to-and-fro of people parting and time passing pivoted above a deeper force-field of myth and archetype. In the lee of ancient trade winds, modern container ships ply quotidian cargoes. In the back streets of cities, money changes hands in informal currency markets that occupy the sites of centuries-old souks. Out in the Atlantic, travellers make their bleary passage, like many before them, to the shores of the 'new world'. Through the narrows of the Bosphorus, ships pass in the night down the overworked channel that was once the border of 'East' and 'West', a fault-line between competing civilisations. Even in the airport, that icon of supermodernity, and a living symbol of how modern technology has furthered the illusion of transcending physical and geographical boundaries, echoes of the past recur. At the gate, passengers queue to submit themselves to x-ray searches like supplicants seeking the safety of a citadel. Colliding the old with the new, and the strange with the familiar, Çavuşoğlu discloses the subtle nuances and delicate tensions of a world in restless motion, in which people are brought increasingly closer together but, occasionally, sent flying ever further apart.

This publication highlights five of Ergin Çavuşoğlu's multi-screen installations, including a new work, *Point of Departure*, commissioned by Film and Video Umbrella and Northern Gallery for Contemporary Art, Sunderland. Like the artist's single-channel pieces (which are not covered in the scope of this book but which are just as worthy of similar attention), they testify not only to Çavuşoğlu's uncanny eye for detail, but to the consummate visual poetry that lies at the heart of so much of his work. I would like to relay my thanks to Alistair Robinson at Northern Gallery for Contemporary Art for his role in co-commissioning *Point of Departure* and to Pernilla Holmes and Matt Watkins at Haunch of Venison in London for their contribution towards that work and this accompanying book. I am grateful also to the Henry Moore Foundation (for their additional funding of the project) and the University of Portsmouth (for their significant support of the publication); to my colleagues at Film and Video Umbrella, and the writers, Claire Doherty, Chris Darke and Simon Harvey, for their excellent texts.

Finally, though, my thanks are to Ergin Çavuşoğlu, whose input into both the commission and the publication has been unflaggingly generous and good-spirited on the long journey from there to here.

Airport Poetics

Chris Darke

An airport is never *just* an airport. As symbol and site, the airport is witness to the achievement of one of mankind's greatest species-surpassing dreams in the everyday miracle of flight. As such, it has something of the utopian about it but, like all utopian spaces, it carries within itself its opposite, the spectacle of the dream realised as either a banal, instrumental or frightful fact. The history of air travel describes a trajectory from its heroic period in the early days of the twentieth century to the current age of anxiety ('from Lindbergh to Bin Laden' as a cultural historian has put it), during which time the airport has become a global gateway combining the two great preoccupations of the present age: fear and shopping.[1] Everyone is familiar with the attendant rituals and atmosphere of the modern airport. Make your way through the throat of the security check, fold your coat, unload keys and mobile phone, submit to electromagnetic scan and manual pat-down, and pray that your face is in favour with the database lest you find yourself being spirited towards some unmarked plane standing ready for 'rendition'. Gravitate down long neon corridors of moving walkways towards the fingers of flight departure, musing all the while on how the processing of people replicates, on a different scale, the handling of baggage.[2]

Ergin Çavuşoğlu's video installation *Point of Departure* is concerned less with flight than with the rites of passage involved in air travel, the dead time of check-in and baggage scans, the busy waiting in the sterile zones of cafés and departure lounges. It is a work that explores the airport both as an architectural structure, a machine for processing travellers and their belongings, but also as a space that lends itself to a certain *poetic* treatment. While it is tempting to conceive of the airport in an abstract Platonic sense, it is important to acknowledge that, in its delineation of certain characteristics of 'airport-*ness*', Çavuşoğlu's work departs from footage shot in two specific airports, Stansted in the south of England and Trabzon in the Turkish Black Sea region.

Facing each other from the opposite edges of the European landmass, these two locations are subtly separated and recombined in *Point of Departure*. The first images that appear across all six of the installation's carefully arranged screens are static shots of airport security gates and baggage scanners. Through their emphasis on linear composition and foreclosed space, these shots do not tell us where we are, other than in the generic 'non-place' of the airport and, at this point in the work, the sound-mix also contributes to this generalised airport ambience. Gradually, as the work unwinds across the screens, we notice details of colour, dress and language that identify the two locations as different, and two travellers in particular are paid special attention by Çavuşoğlu's camera. A distinct, unchanging set of images unwinds throughout the work: a series of x-ray scans ('tomograms') of baggage as it passes through the CAT scanner, images that take on an emblematic status.[3] We also become aware of the two different locations as spaces that, while geographically distant from each other, are presented here as being almost contiguous and giving onto another, much larger, abstract space that lies beyond the architecture of the piece even while being alluded to by it. One way of interpreting *Point of Departure*, then, is as a work seeking to elaborate a 'poetics of space' for the airport.

Space is never *just* space, least of all if the space in question happens to be that of an airport. Since the inception, in the 1980s, of the so-called 'spatial turn' in human geography and social theory, the critical conception of space, or 'spatiality', has extended well beyond the now defunct project of post-modernism in which it once participated to inform the humanities and arts in general. It is, without question, one of the key concepts of the times through whose application the spirit of the age might be, if not revealed, then at least imagined. To invoke a 'poetics of space' is to allude to certain key ideas proposed by writers whose influence is fundamental, if only at the level of metaphorical suggestiveness. For example, there is of course Borges's short story of 1945, *The Aleph*, referred to as the greatest metaphor for the impossibility of language, in its sequential progression, describing geography, where things are 'stubbornly simultaneous'.[4] Equally significant is Gaston Bachelard's seminal 1958 study *La poétique de l'espace*, in which the philosopher of science presented a study of poetically charged domestic spaces such as the attic and cellar, the drawer, chest and cabinet. The Italian phenomenological philosopher Gianni Vattimo, too, has offered a compelling reading of this idea of 'the poetic' as regards space in relationship to Heidegger. Vattimo addresses Heidegger's quotation of lines from Hölderlin:

> Voll Verdienst, doch dichterish, wohnet
> Der Mensch auf dieser Erde
>
> Full of merit, yet poetically, man
> Dwells on this earth[5]

While one might now find Vattimo's argument debatable (he reads Heidegger's account of Hölderlin in terms of the transition from modernity to post-modernity), he nevertheless has useful things to say regarding the phrase 'yet poetically man/Dwells on this earth':

> To dwell poetically does not mean to dwell in such a way that one needs poetry, but to dwell with a sensitivity to the poetic, characterised by the impossibility, in a sense, of defining clear-cut boundaries between reality and imagination. If there is a passage from modernity to post-

1 Alastair Gordon, *Naked Airport: a Cultural History of the World's Most Revolutionary Structure*, Metropolitan Books, New York, 2004, p.232.

2 'Fingers' and 'throats' are terms used by architects to designate these areas.

3 Computerised Axial Tomography (CAT) is used in both medical imaging and security systems. The CAT scanner is a hollow tube that surrounds an object, bombards it with x-rays and records the resulting data. The CAT scanner uses this data to create a detailed 'tomogram', or slice, of the object in question. In the case of baggage scanning, the CAT scan is able to calculate the mass and density of individual objects within the baggage based on the tomogram.

4 See, for example, Edward W. Soja, *Postmodern Geographies: The Reassertion of Space in Critical Social Theory*, Verso, London & New York, 1989, p.2.

5 Gianni Vattimo, 'The End of Modernity, The End of the Project?' in *Rethinking Architecture: A reader in cultural theory*, Neil Leach [Ed.], Routledge, London and New York, 1997, p.148.

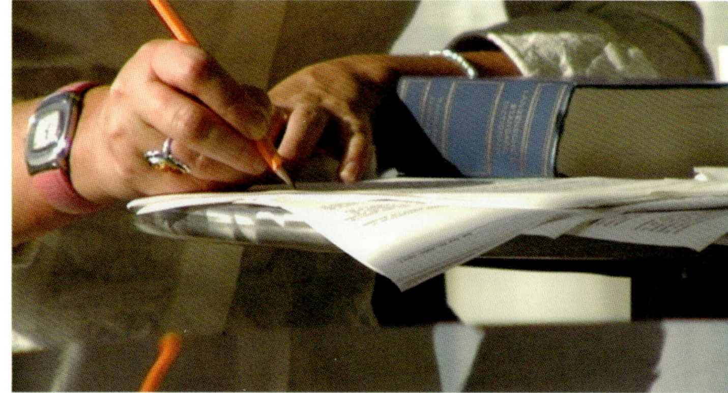

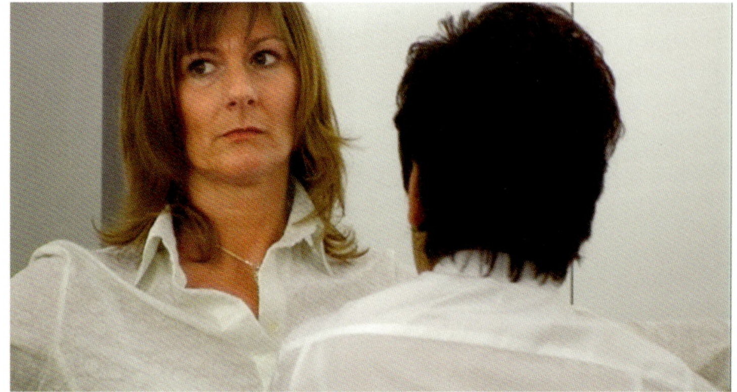

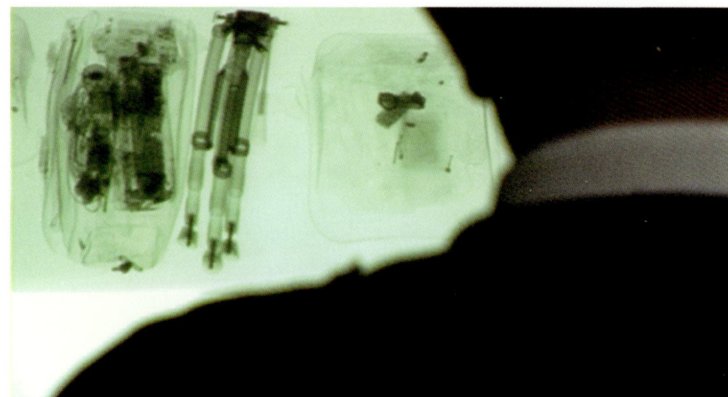

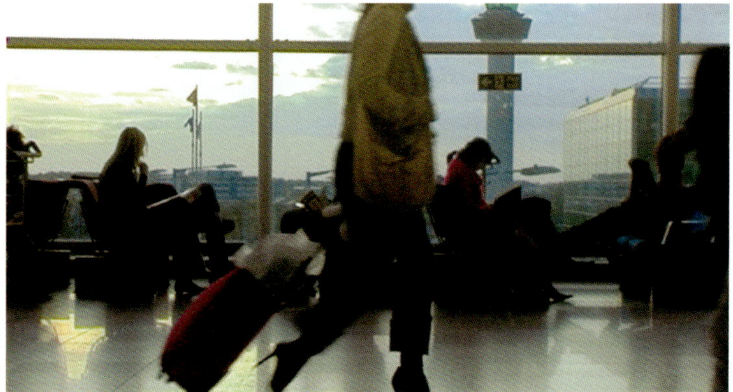

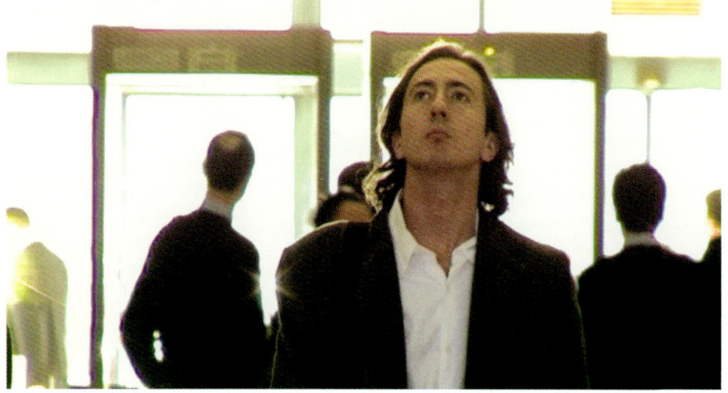

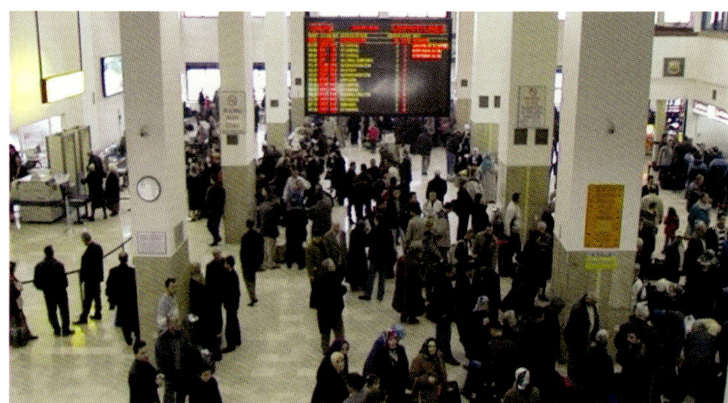

Point of Departure (2006)

> modernity, it seems to lie in a wearing away of the boundaries between the real and the unreal or, at the very least, in a wearing away of the boundaries of the *real*. [...] Contemporary history is that phase of history in which everything tends to be presented in the form of simultaneity.[6]

A characteristic of this poetic apprehension of space is the recognition of its Aleph-like capacity to embody 'much in little' (at one point in Borges's fable the insufferable poet and keeper of the magical Aleph, Carlos Argentino Daneri, proclaims the Latin phrase '*multum in parvo!*') It is evident, too, in the will to detect natural forms in man-made structures, as Bachelard does in *Poetics of Space*, or the ancient in the modern, as in Virilio's description of the ancestral structure of the city gate being replaced by the airport security gate. One might go further and suggest that the poetic approach supplies figures and motifs by which it becomes possible to imagine particular spatial configurations in relation to the wider world, of which they are metonymic: for example, the relationship between, as Bachelard puts it, 'the house and the universe' where the house can contain a universe even while being contained by the universe. The ambition that is evident in Çavușoğlu's installation (impossibly overreaching, it has to be said, but still valuable and paradoxically modest in its execution) is to create a structure by which one might begin to imagine the world. But where does one start in this wish to embody totality? Where does one find a point of departure? If a house can become the universe then, surely, in the anxious environment of the present age, can the airport not become the world?

Point of Departure can be seen to be a work about space *per se*; that is, the experience and condition of contemporary globalised space as the relationship between specific *places*: the airports of Stansted and Trabzon, the installation itself and the space of its exhibition. This movement from the general to the particular, from space to place, is not constructed by the work as a set of oppositions (space *versus* place etc) but as a series of imbrications, each being contained within and acting as a function of the other. Two images in Çavuşoğlu's installation have a 'poetic' function that bears this out, those that show security gates and 'tomograms' of luggage as it moves through the scanner. They function to send the spectator-participant shuttling backwards and forwards from the realm of the real to the realm of the imagination and back again, from the world of the airport to the structure of the installation to the space of exhibition, and beyond, and back, again and again. The 'gate' is itself doubled in the work, featuring as an image and an element of the structure of the *dispositif*. The images of Trabzon and Stansted airports obsessively document the functioning and the protocol of the security gates (a process that is noticeably more rigorous at the English end than it is at the Turkish) and the attention paid to the form and function of such gates cannot but remind one of Paul Virilio's seminal diagnosis in 'The Overexposed City' in which he describes how, since the 1960s, the city is no longer governed by physical boundaries but by systems of electronic surveillance; in 'the exo-city' the gateway gives way to the security gate at the airport:

> From here on, constructed space occurs within an electronic topology where the framing of perspective and the gridwork weft of numerical images renovate the division of urban property. The ancient private/public occultation and the distinction between housing and traffic are replaced by an overexposure in which the difference between 'near' and 'far' simply ceases to exist [...] The representation of the modern city can no longer depend on the ceremonial opening of gates, nor on the ritual processions and parades lining the streets and avenues with spectators. From here on, urban architecture has to work with the opening of a new 'technological space-time'. In terms of access, telematics replaces the doorway. The sound of gates gives way to the clatter of data banks and the rites of passage of a technical culture whose progress is disguised by the immateriality of its parts and networks... Where once one necessarily entered the city by means of a physical gateway, now one passes through an *audiovisual protocol* in which the methods of audience and surveillance have transformed even the forms of public greeting and daily reception.[7]

In processing people and their baggage, these gates produce images as an adjunct to one's passport, a kind of 'Open Sesame!' (It no longer is enough that one's papers are, in the old-fashioned phrase, found to be 'in order'; one's images too must be in order). These images are therefore part of the gate, part of its structure and protocol and, so, Çavuşoğlu incorporates them into his work. He does so with a sly but telling inversion. At the heart of the installation's architecture, which is also its 'entrance', two screens are suspended above the floor exactly facing each other and between them the CAT scan images are projected onto the floor. This combination of two facing screens and the floor-projection forms an approximation of a gateway whose arch is inverted. Again, Virilio comes to mind:

> In this new perspective devoid of horizon, the city was entered not through a gate nor through an *arc de triomphe*, but rather through an electronic audience system.[8]

This arrangement of elements produces an interesting effect of interdiction; true to its shape of an inverted arch, it declares 'Do Not Enter' and it is

6 *ibid.* p.149.
7 Paul Virilio, 'The Overexposed City' in Leach, p.383.
8 *ibid.*, p.382.

surprising to see how few visitors to the installation dare, or deem it acceptable, to step over, into and across the CAT scan images. *Point of Departure* is therefore not an environment that one moves within, but around which one orbits, stacked like airliners, busy waiting like passengers.

This image could be said to function as the work's heraldic *mise-en-abyme*: the bags containing objects are themselves contained as they pass through the scanner. Likewise, the work itself has certain features (six screens, documentary images of its two locations, 'character-types' who introduce a certain horizon of fictional meaning) contained by its own spatial integrity as an installation (with the inverted gate at its core), itself contained within the larger space of exhibition. Both images (the gateways, the CAT scans) are therefore materialised in the form of the installation, they move from the space of the screen to contribute to embodying the work itself. This migration from one space to another is of a part with the work's subject as well as its method and speaks of the movement within and between the work's three levels of space: that of the image, that of the architectural form of the installation and that of the place it occupies within the space of exhibition (which the sound-mix helps sculpt).

Something needs to be said about the passengers we see milling about in the airport footage, in which a man and a woman come to our attention. In fact, we can't help but notice them. There is something in their lightly worn self-consciousness that draws our eyes to them, this sleek duo of departure lounge-lizards; a quality about them that tells us they are actors: 'He', with his long aristocratic face and slightly leonine swagger; 'She', blonde and busy rewriting a typescript at her café table. Together, they perform cameos of what the political economist Susan George has called the 'international fast caste', frequent flyers and privileged migrants at the opposite end of globalisation's food chain from the refugees and neo-liberal proletariat. 'She' is a journalist travelling east on an assignment; 'He' is Turkish post-graduate student travelling west — which is as much as we learn about them from the sparse dialogues. But they have a function other than being representative 'types': they serve to draw our attention not only to themselves but also to their surroundings and the people around them; not so much 'characters' but rather what the French would call *figurants*, or 'background artists'. They are there to bring out the background, to set it off, but never to fully separate themselves from it. Çavuşoğlu's decision to emphasise this pair introduces an element of fiction, an imaginary horizon to the locations, the suggestion of a background story to each, but no more than that. They are heading in different directions, their paths crossing *en route* to different destinations. This 'background' is also what hovers ominously behind any depiction of any airport nowadays, the low heavy thud of modernity's migraine, terminal velocity, death from the skies. And the question: what will happen when the fuel runs out? In port cities where the maritime industry has declined, the rivers become the focus for regeneration campaigns, the docks become new temples of cultural tourism or museums of dead industry. Rivers and waterways are geological facts. Despite the territorial weight ascribed to them (think of the concept of 'air space' for example) flight paths are abstractions conceived in thin air. One can readily imagine certain defunct terminals mutating into out-of-town shopping centres, equipped as they already are with malls and cinemas, their duty-free status extinguished, grass pushing through the disused runways. But what of those whose viability has depended on the increase in cheap air travel, itself dependent on the vagaries of the international oil market? Will they become abandoned outposts of the imagination, populated by phantom pilots and ghostly passengers who, like characters from a J.G. Ballard story, take on the stubbornly survivalist attributes of soldiers who don't know that war is over, the last survivors of a dying species?

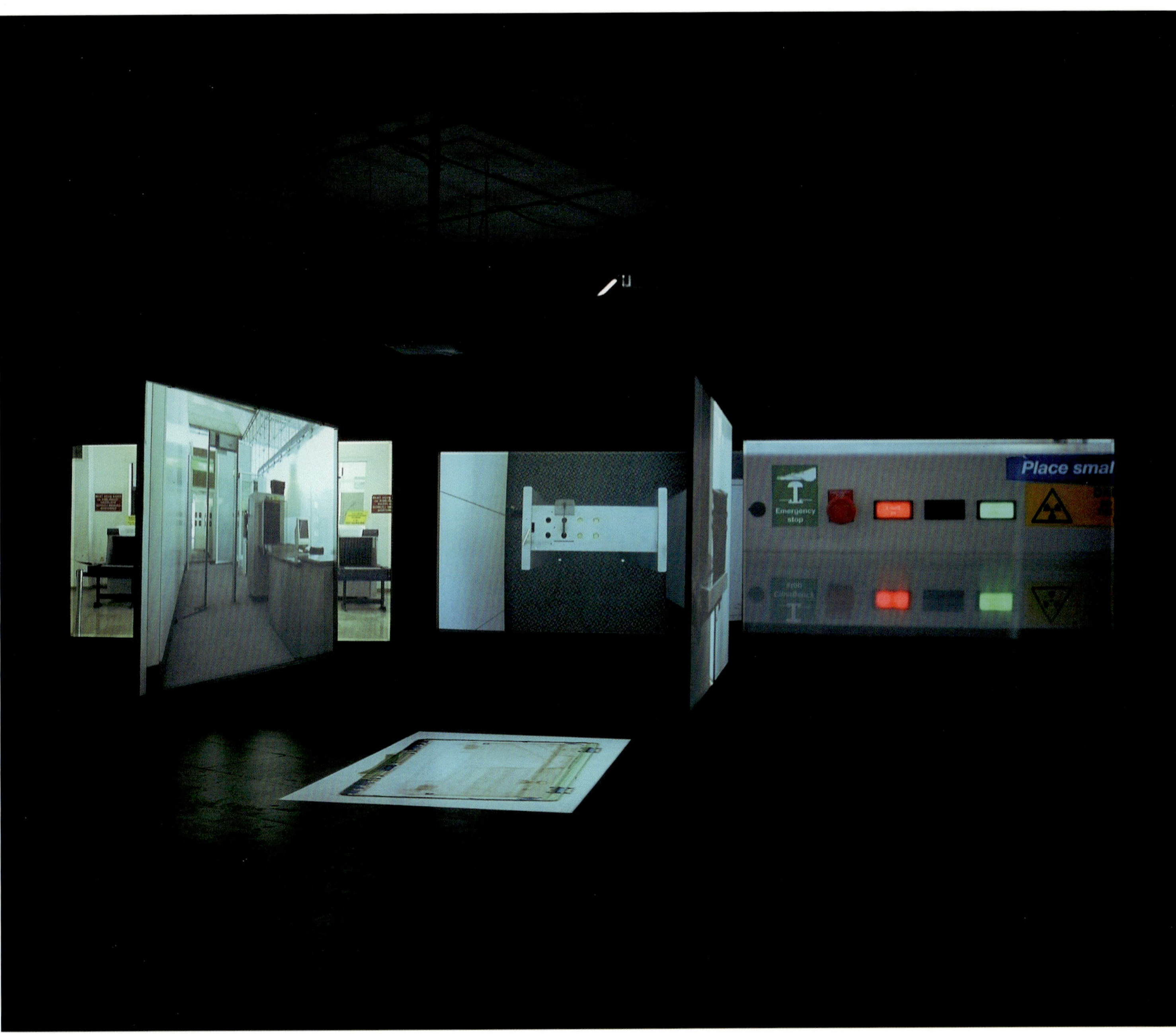

Point of Departure (2006)

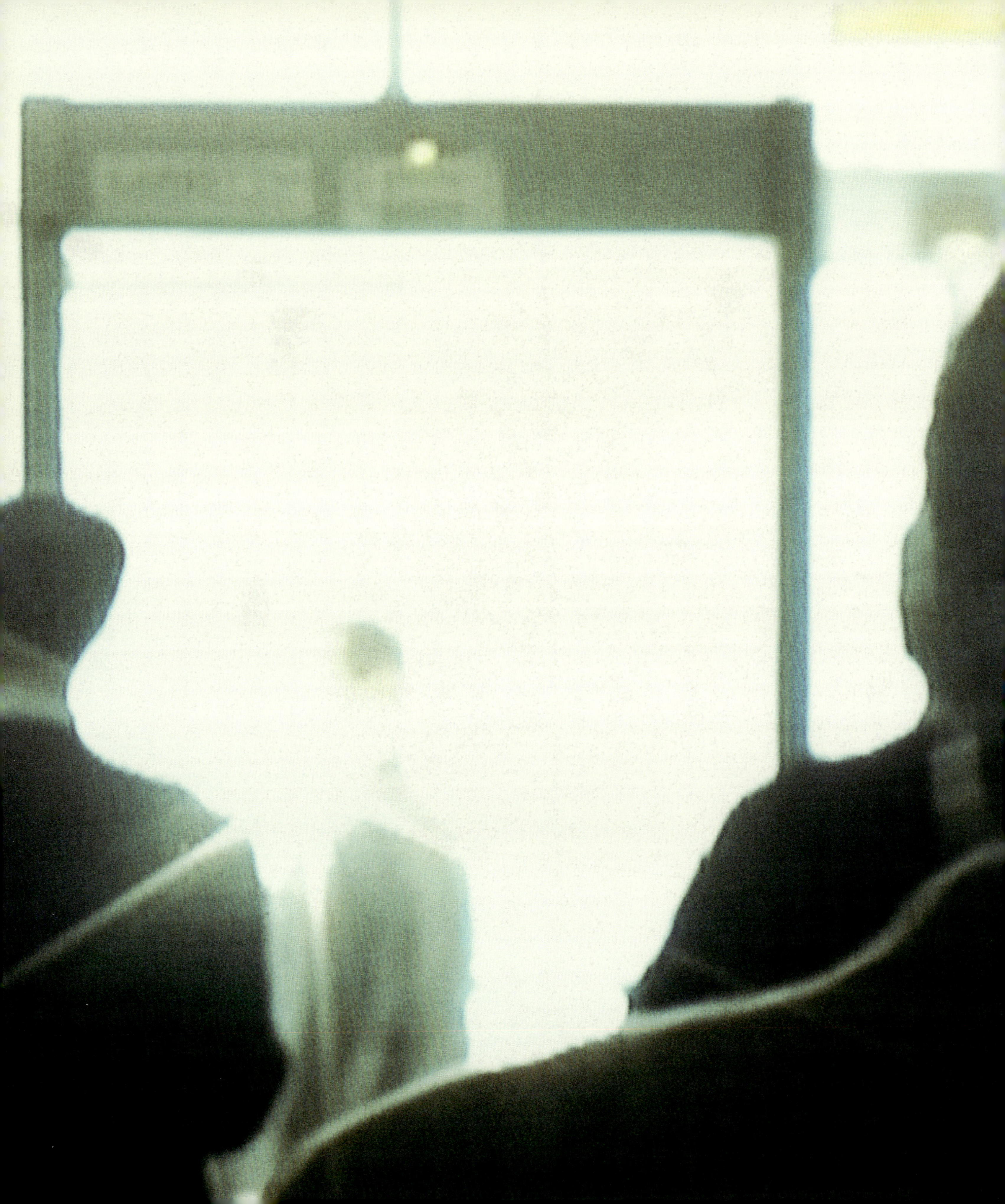

Point of Departure

Point of Departure (2006)
Six-screen video installation, three channels sound
Running time: 31:36min, continuous loop
Dimensions variable: front/rear projection screens
Installation view: Northern Gallery for Contemporary Art, Sunderland, 2006

This is a security announcement! To reduce the number of security alerts, passengers must keep their baggage with them at all times.

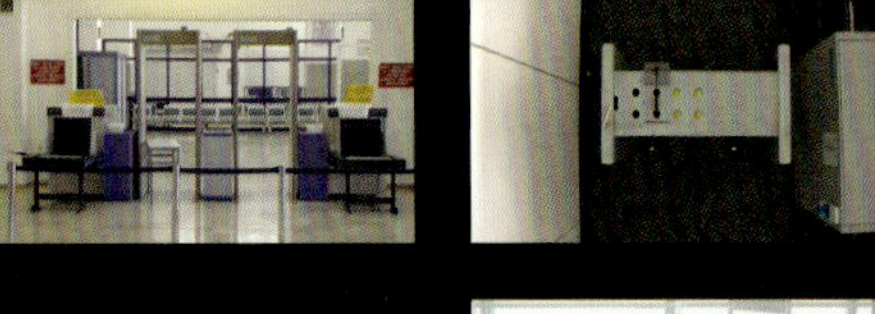
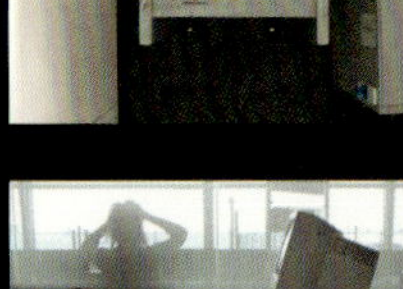
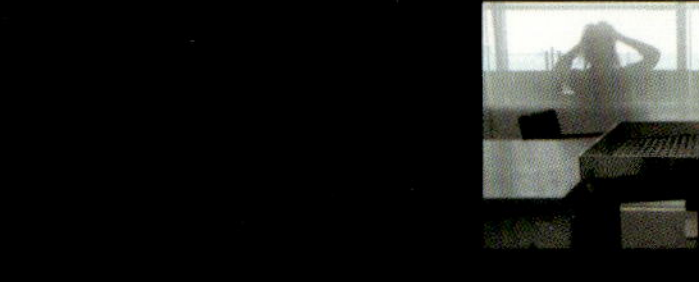
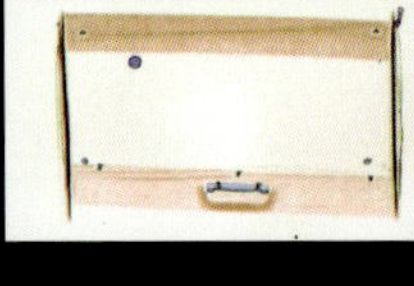
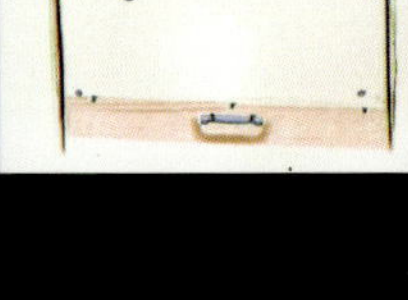

Passengers are reminded that...

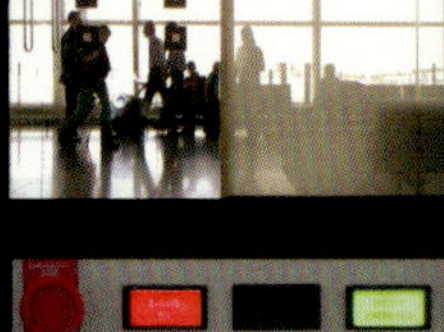
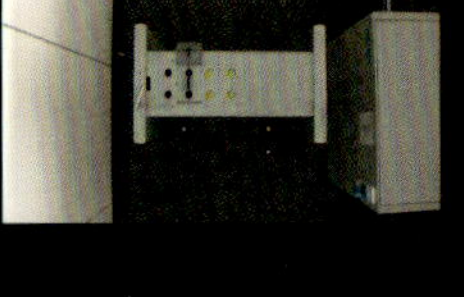
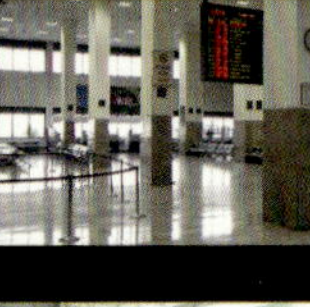
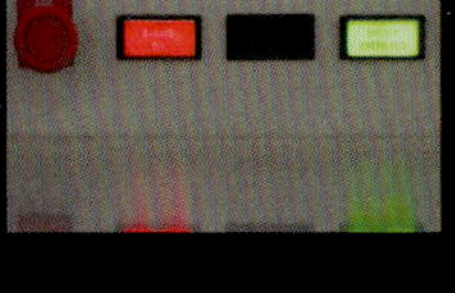
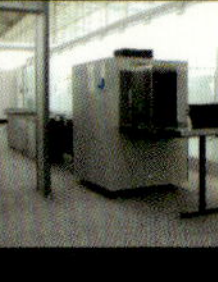

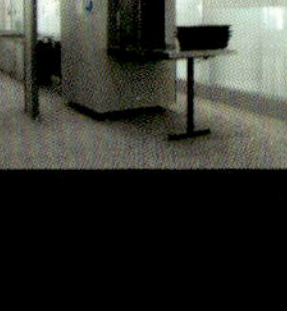
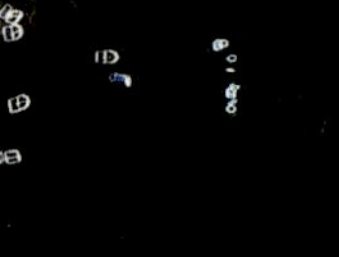

Where you are travelling to? To Poland, actually.
Have a good trip! Thank you. Bye, bye.

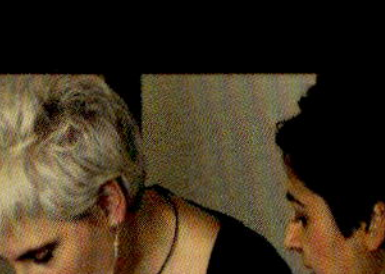
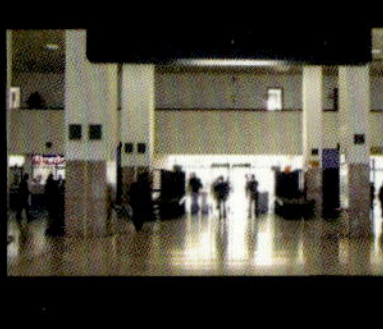
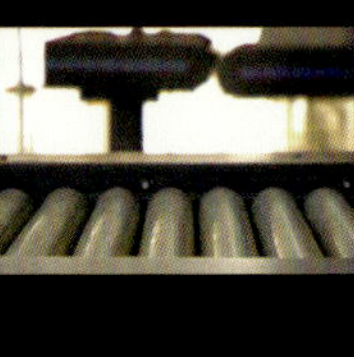
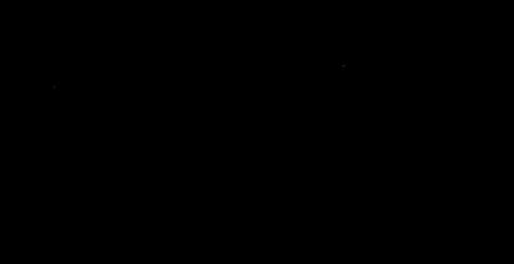

Is there anything sharp in the bag, Sir?
Can I just check the sole of your shoes?

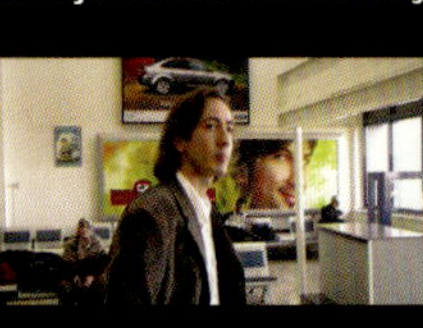
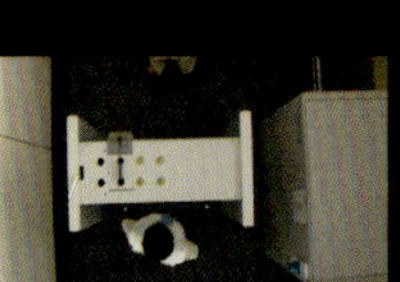
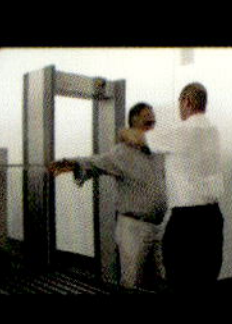
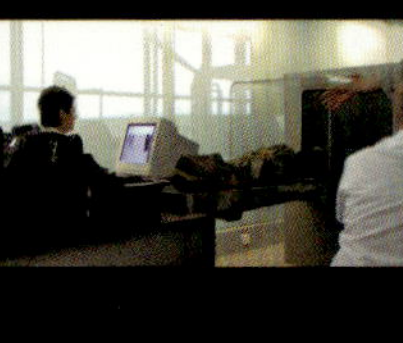
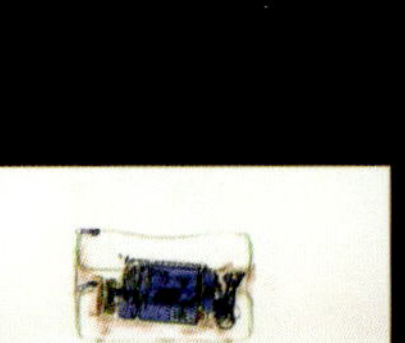
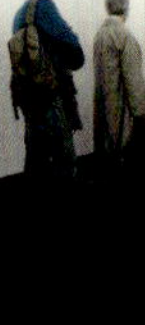

Ben pek sık gelmiyorum artık da unutmuşuz nasıl olduğnu.
Yıllardır devamlı gidip geliyorum, ondan dolayı gayet iyi biliyorum.

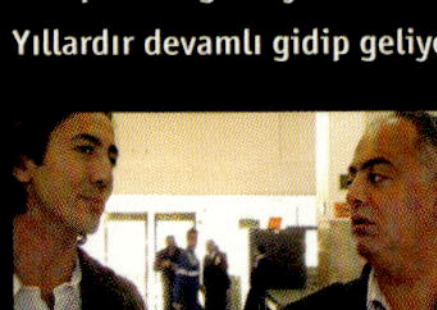
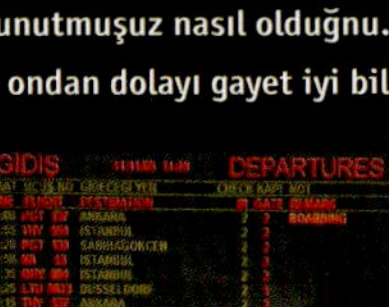
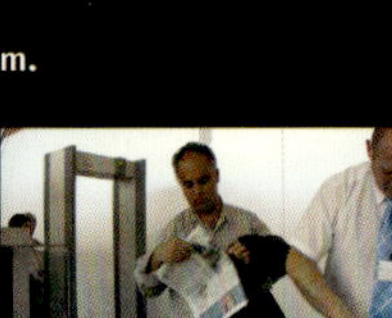
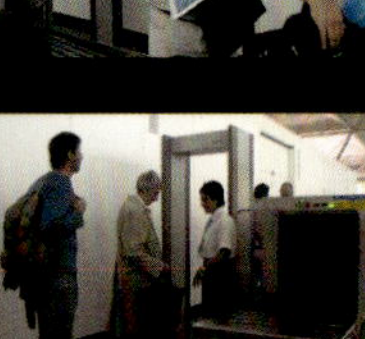
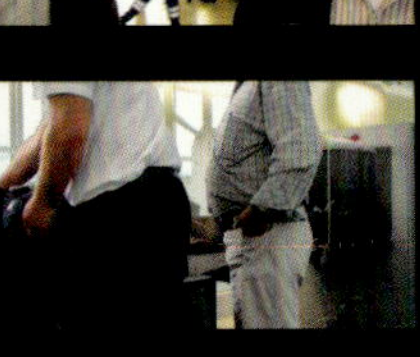
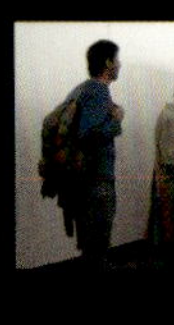
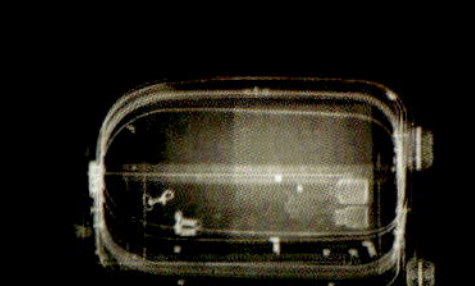

Ceplerinizi boşaltın. Buyurun, buyurun.
Buyurun tek, tek geçelim. Paltonu bu taraftan. Tamam, geçin.

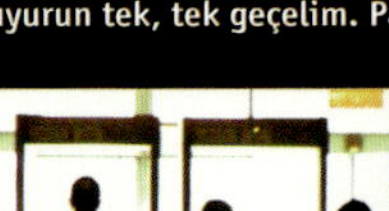

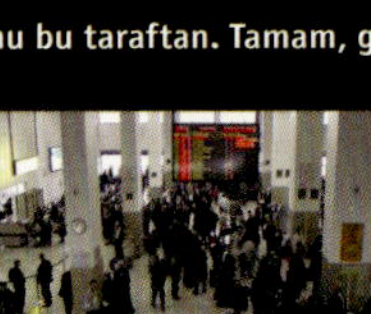
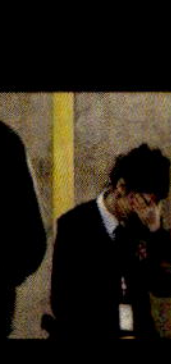
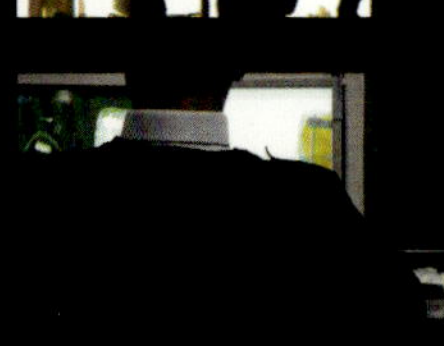

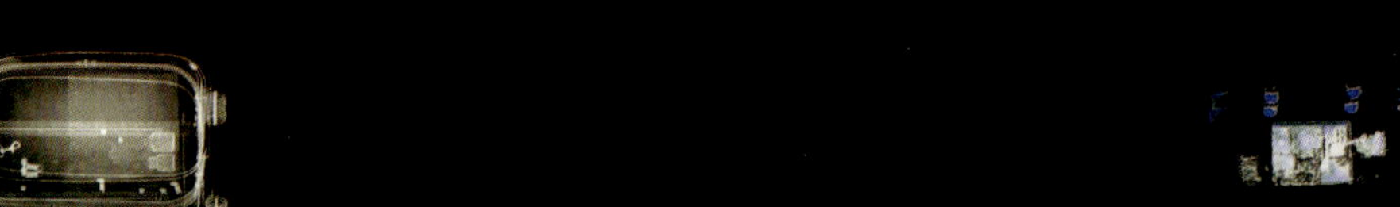

Bir de kül tablası alabilirmiyim? Teşekkürler.
Rica ederim.

Türk Hava Yollarının TK128 Istanbul seferini yapacak yolcularımız. Sayın yolcularımız, güvenlik işlemlerini yaptırmak üzere güvenlik kontrolünden geçmeleri rica olunur.

Easyjet final call for flight EZ255 to Belfast.
Now closing through departure gate 88.

In the early section it says within the boundaries, then it's referring to moving outside the boundaries. Alright, OK, this makes sense. It's basically...

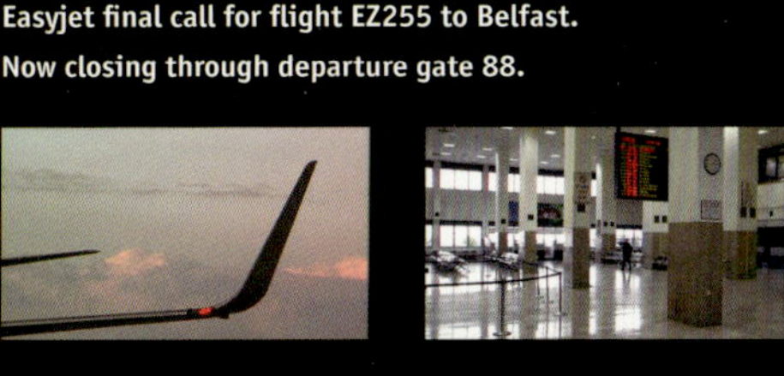

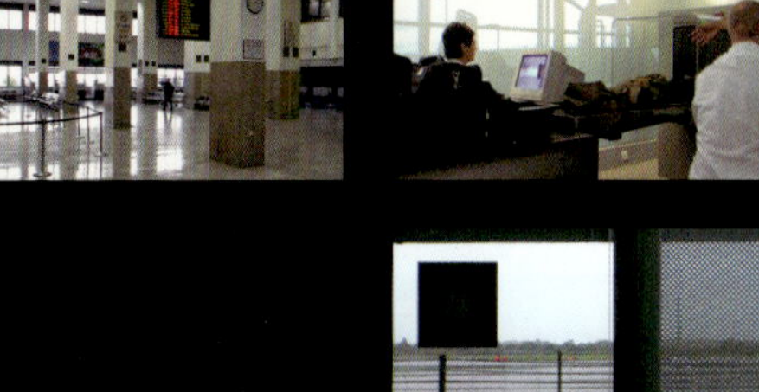

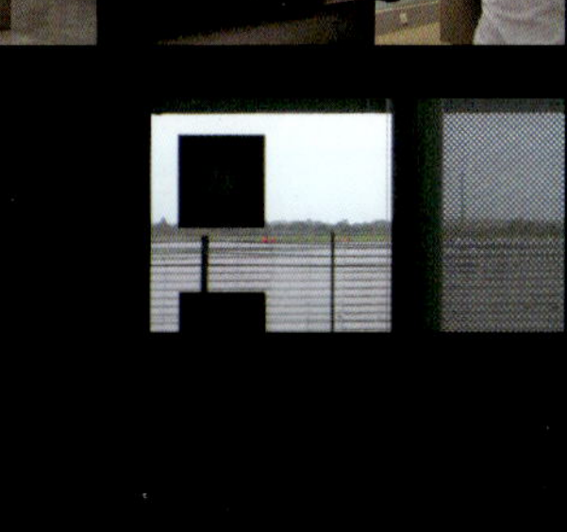

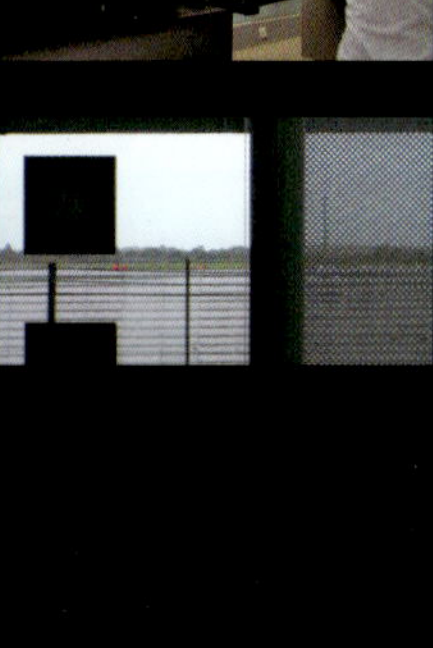

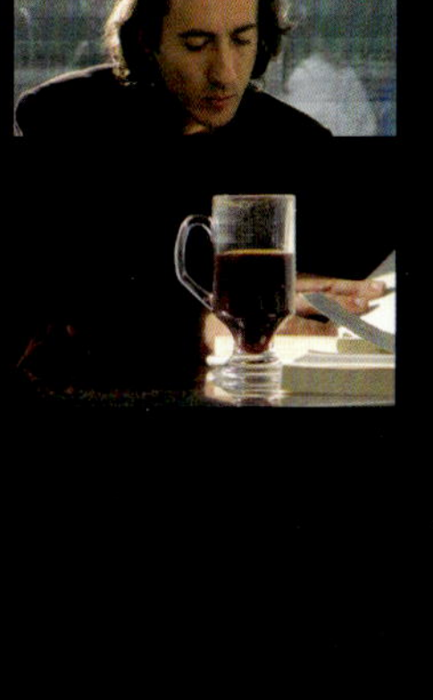

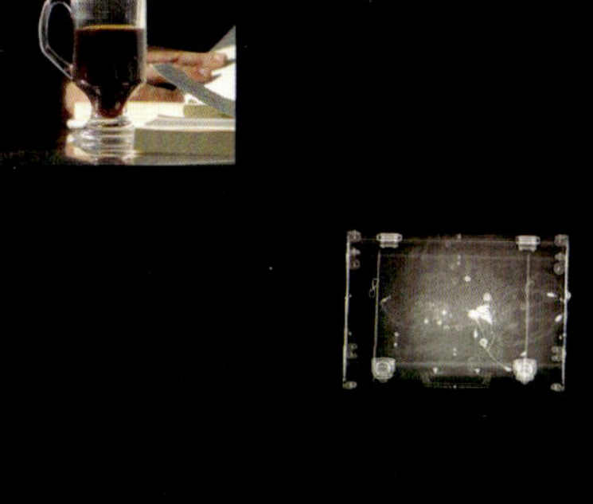

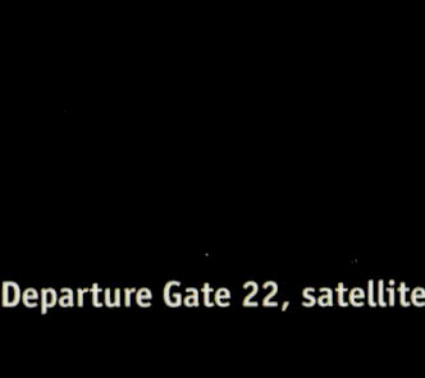

Departure Gate 22, satellite 2...

For your safety and comfort, smoking is not permitted except in the designated areas.
Please refer to smoking area signs.

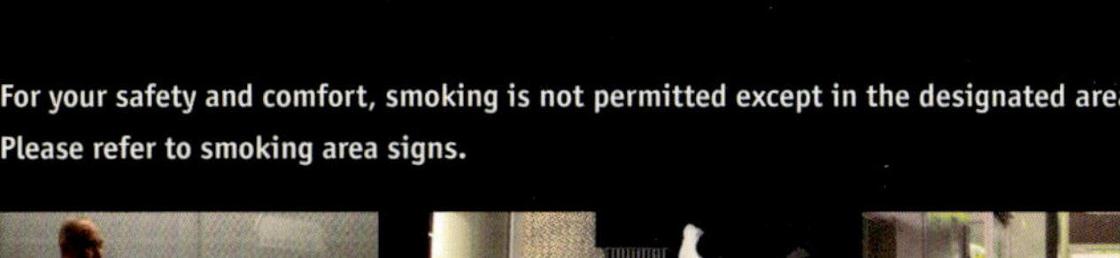

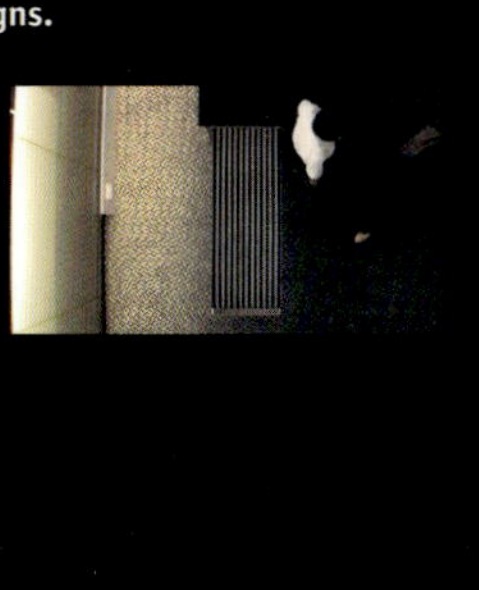

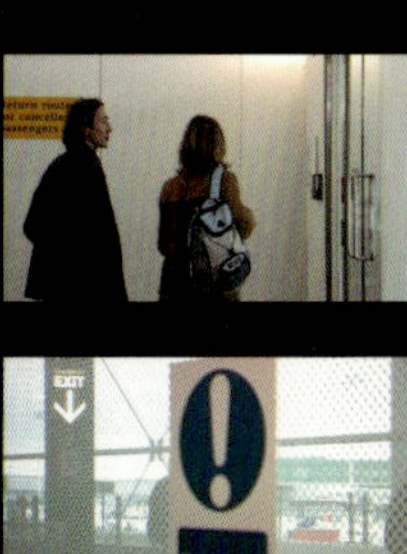

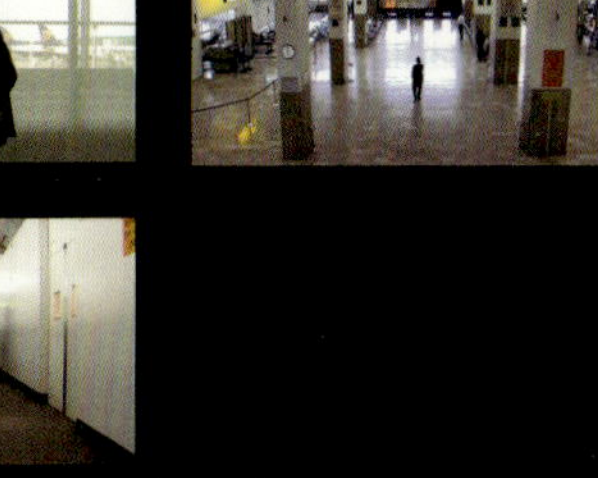

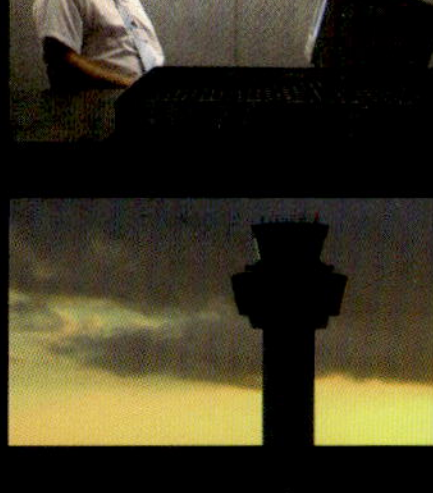

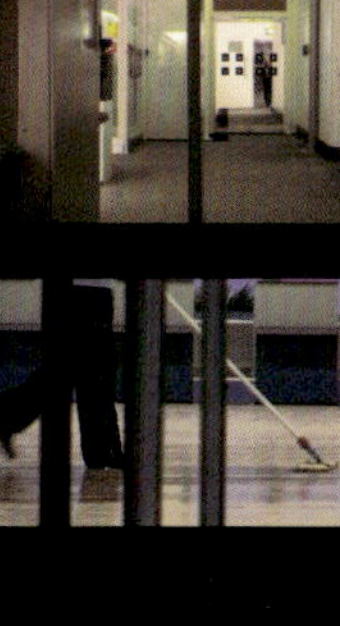

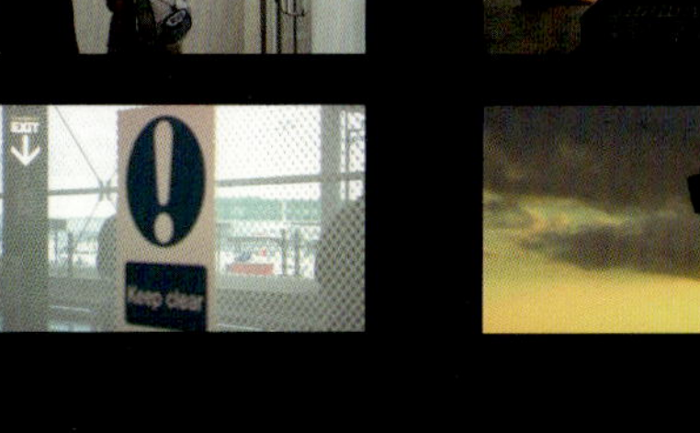

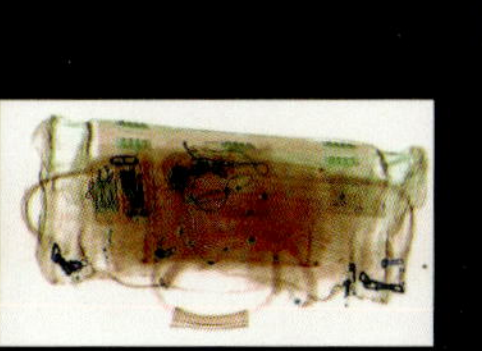

— Are you travelling to Turkey?

— No, I am going to Syria actually, and then to Iraq and Turkey, and then home. How about you, going back home?

— No, I rarely go back nowadays. I'm going further west.

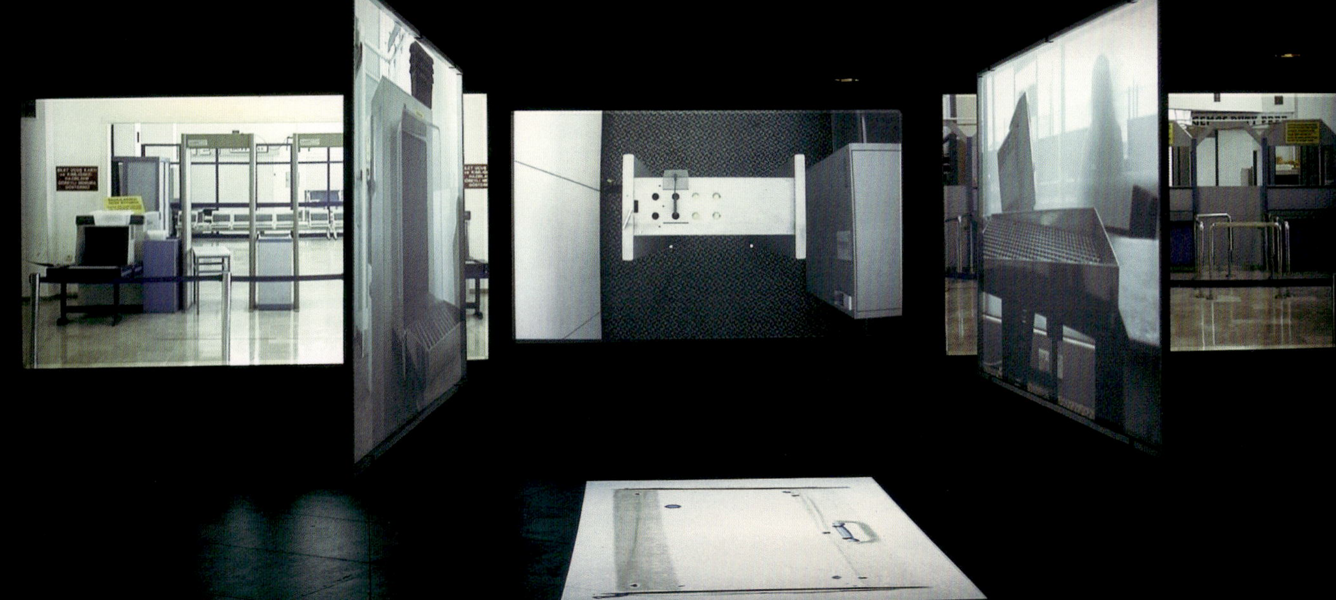

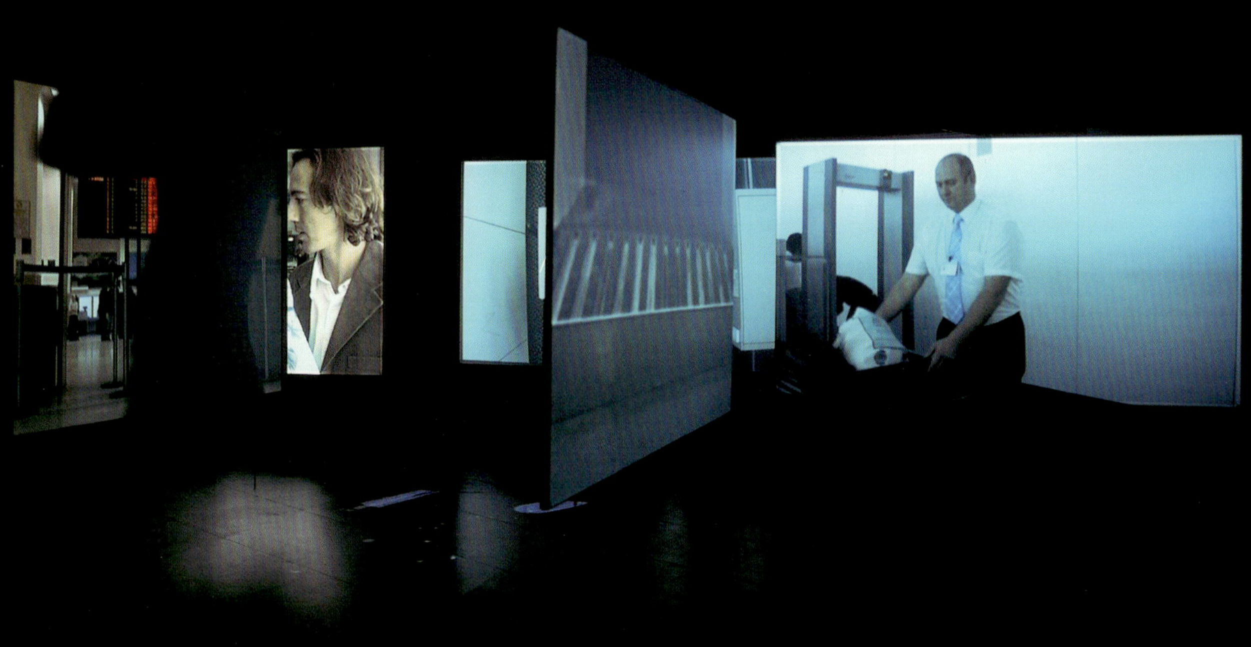

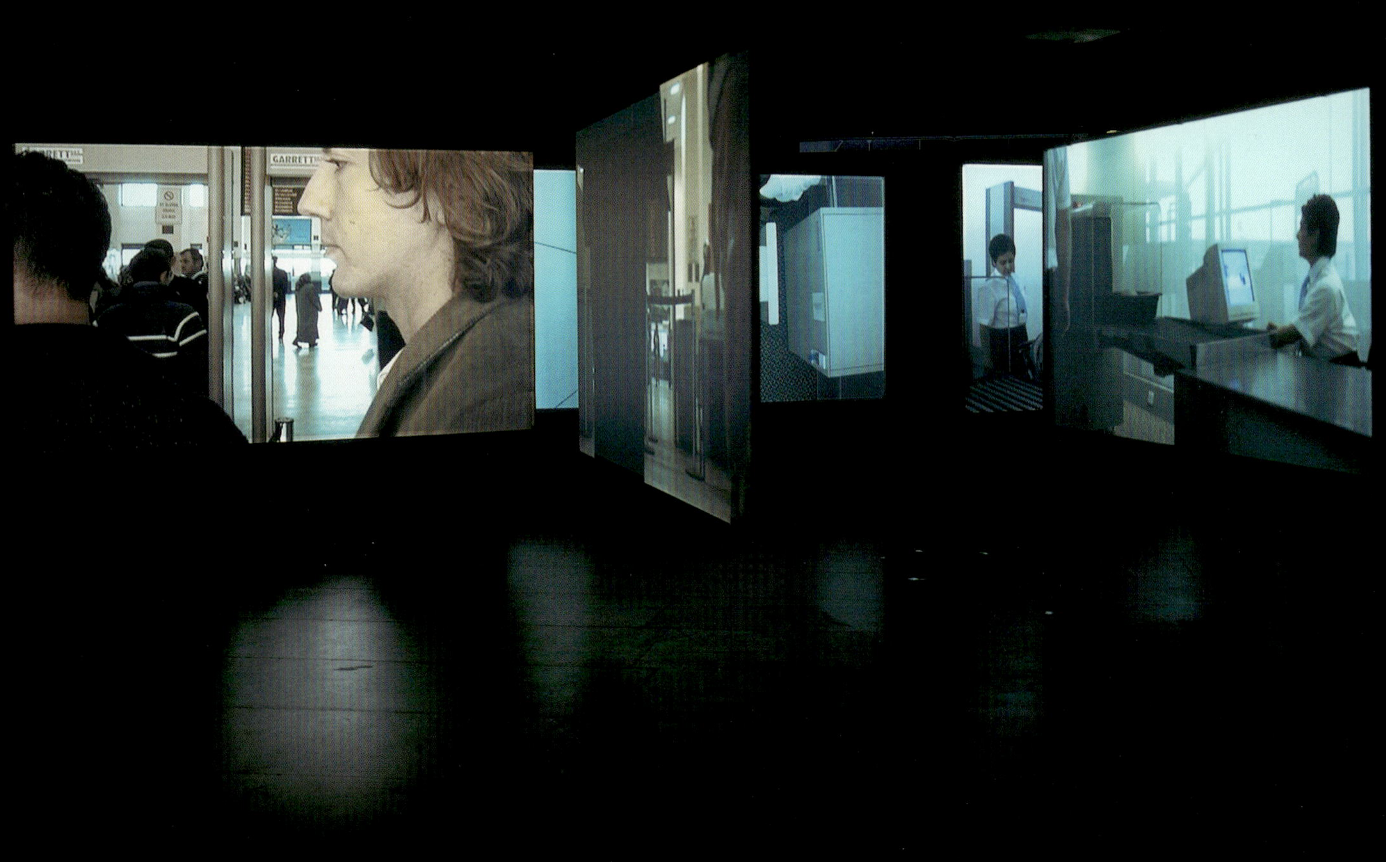

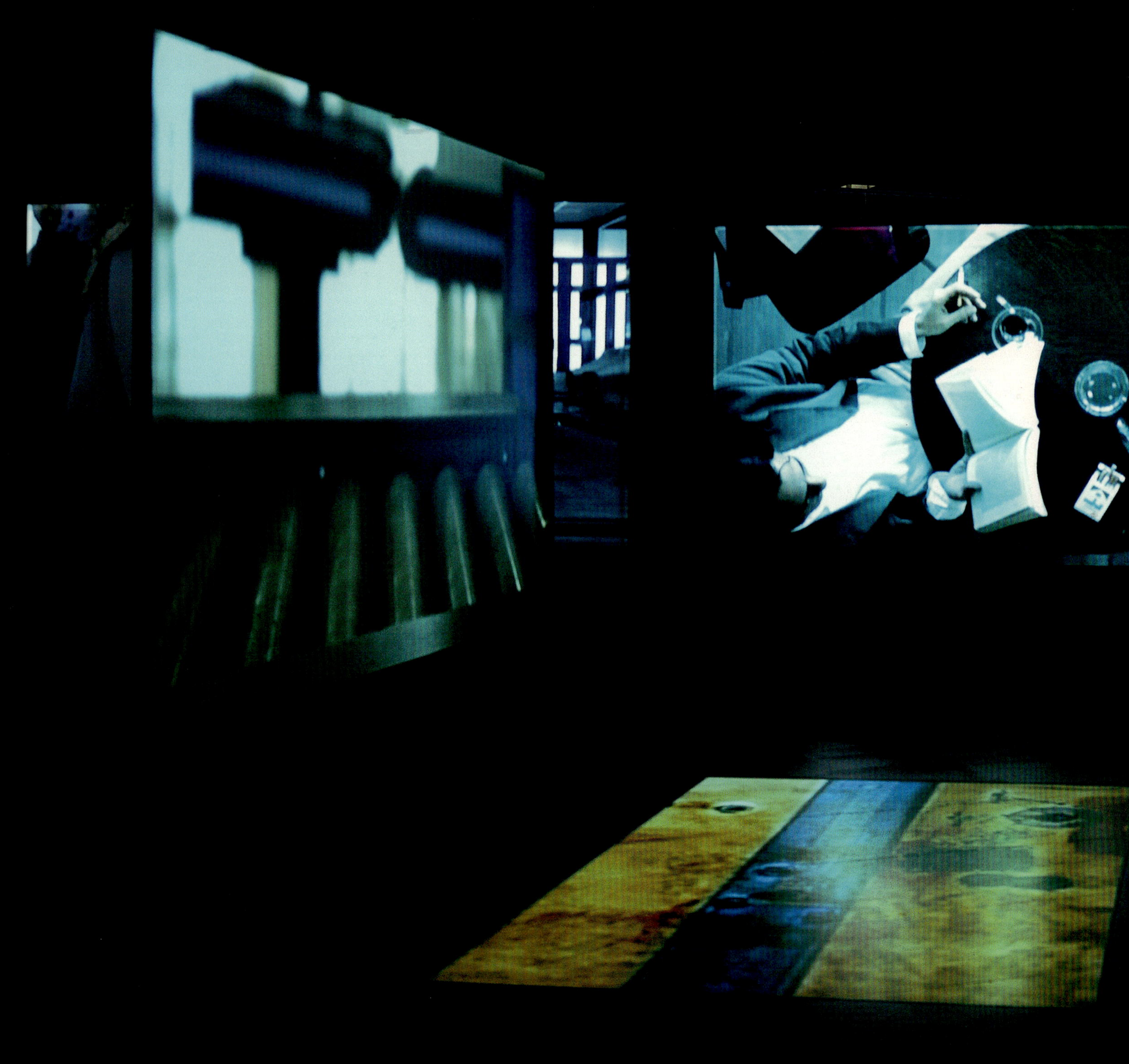

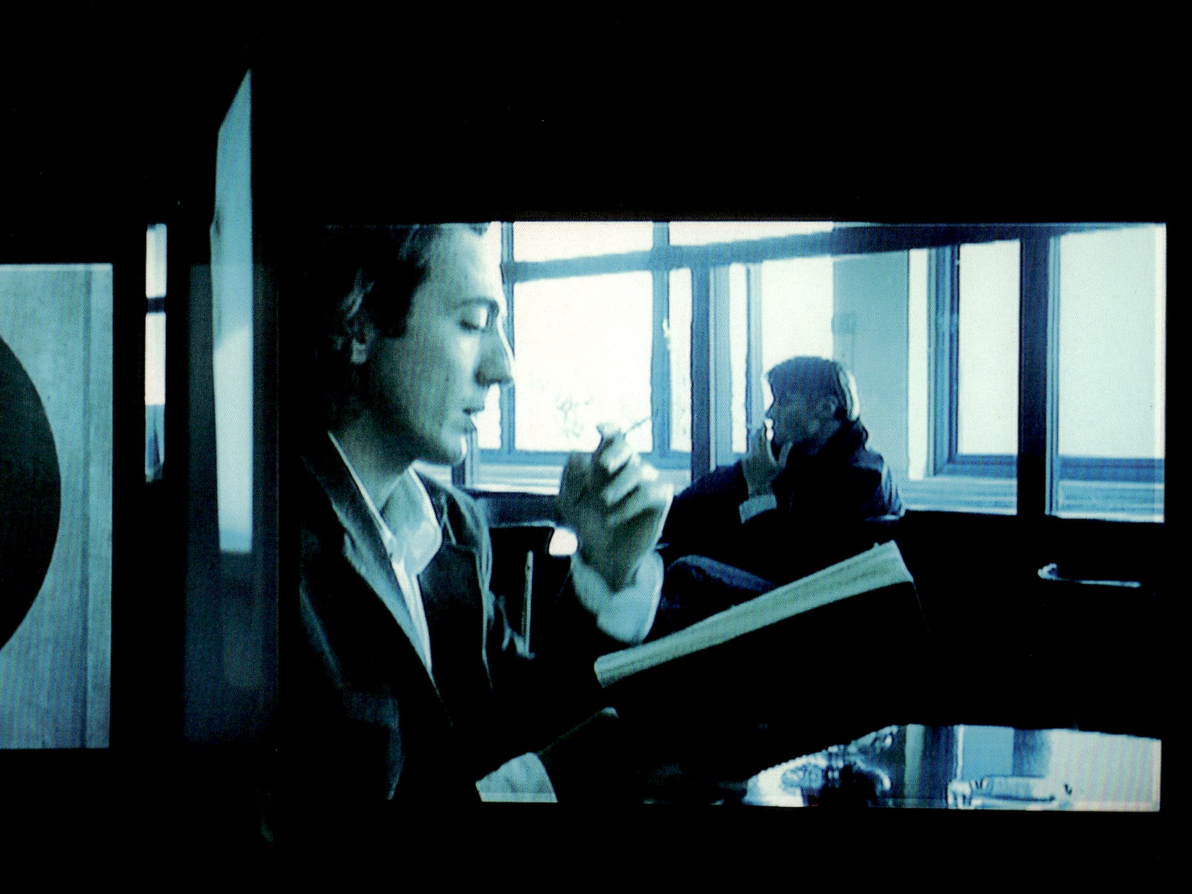

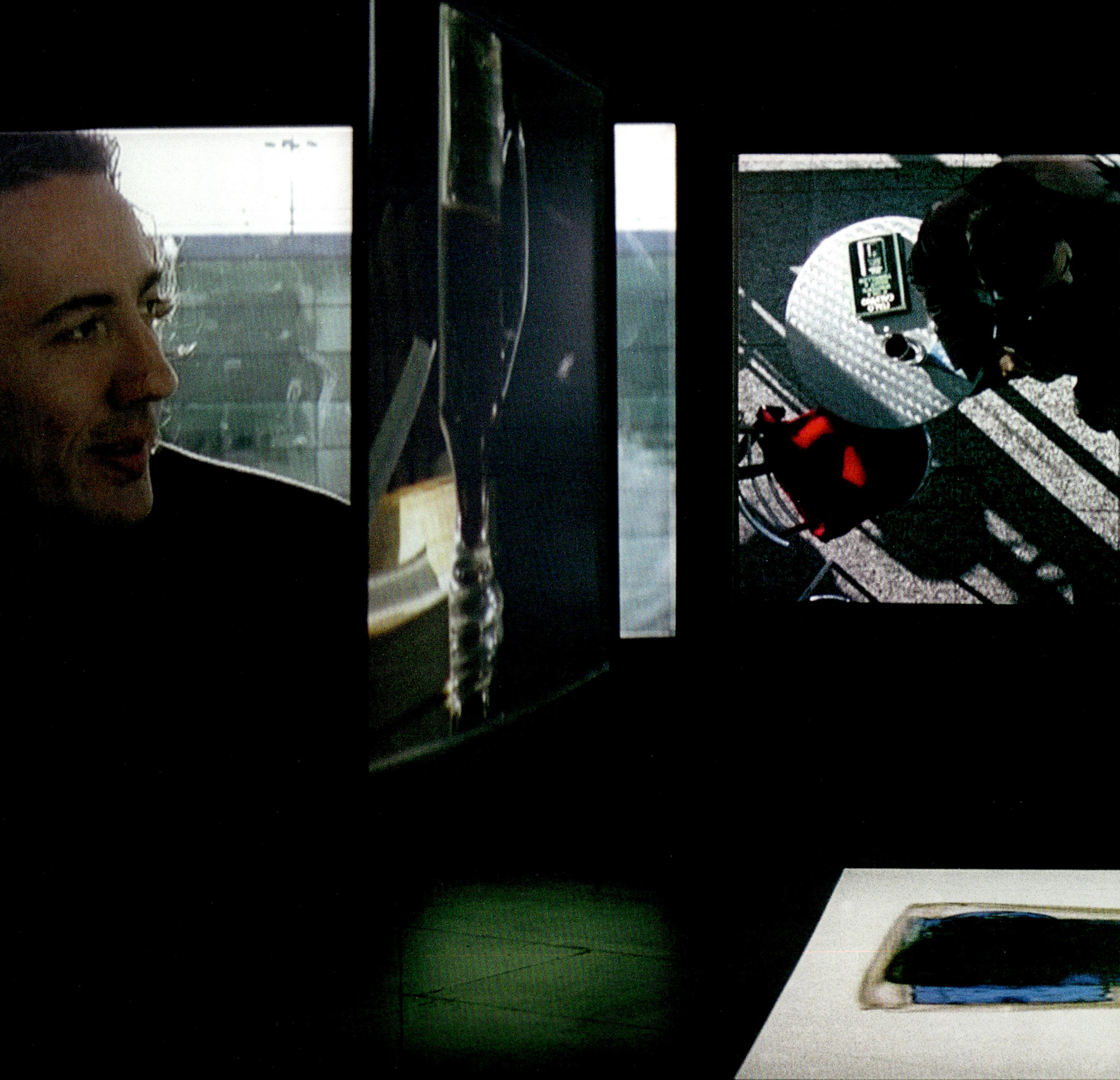

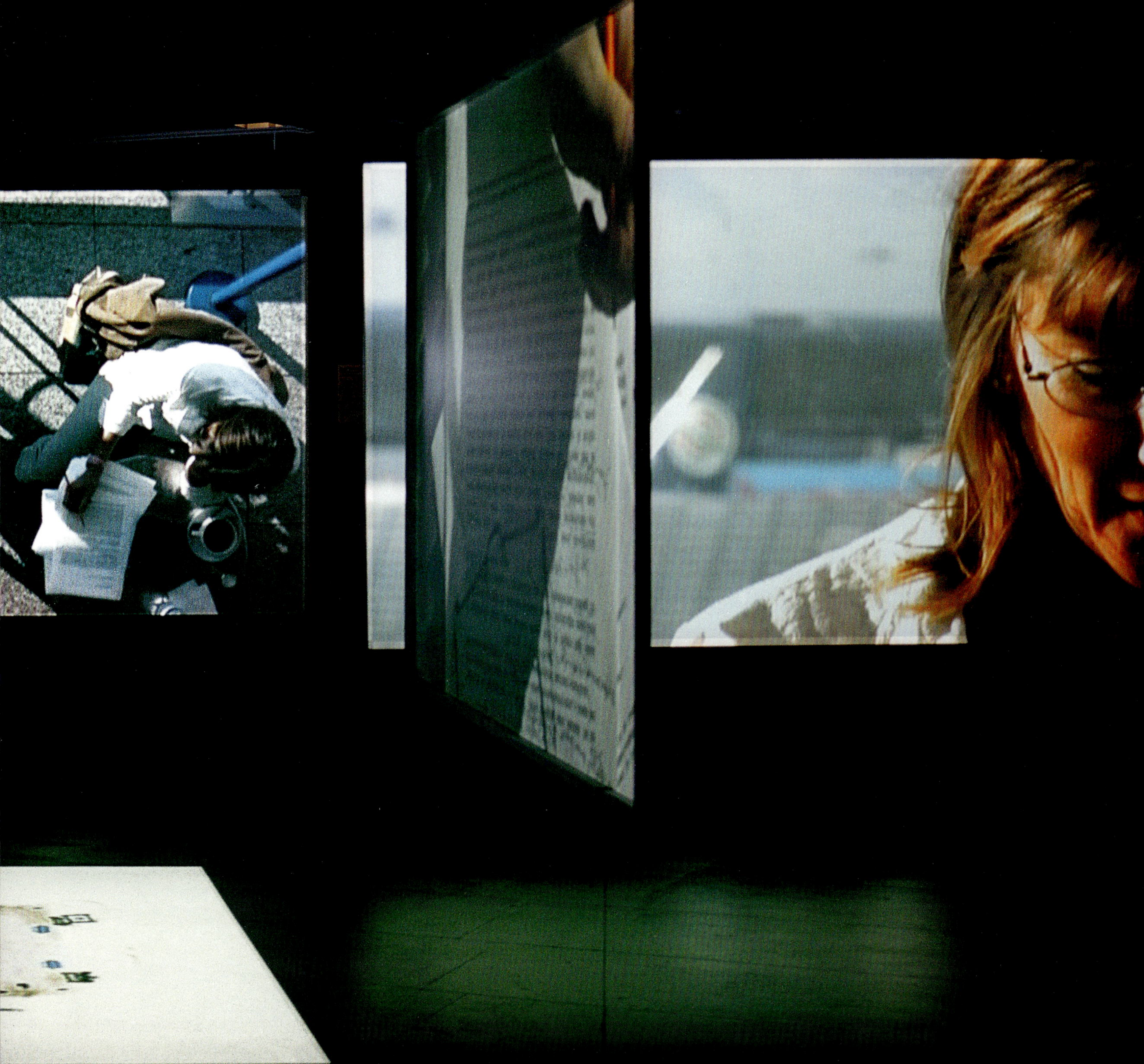

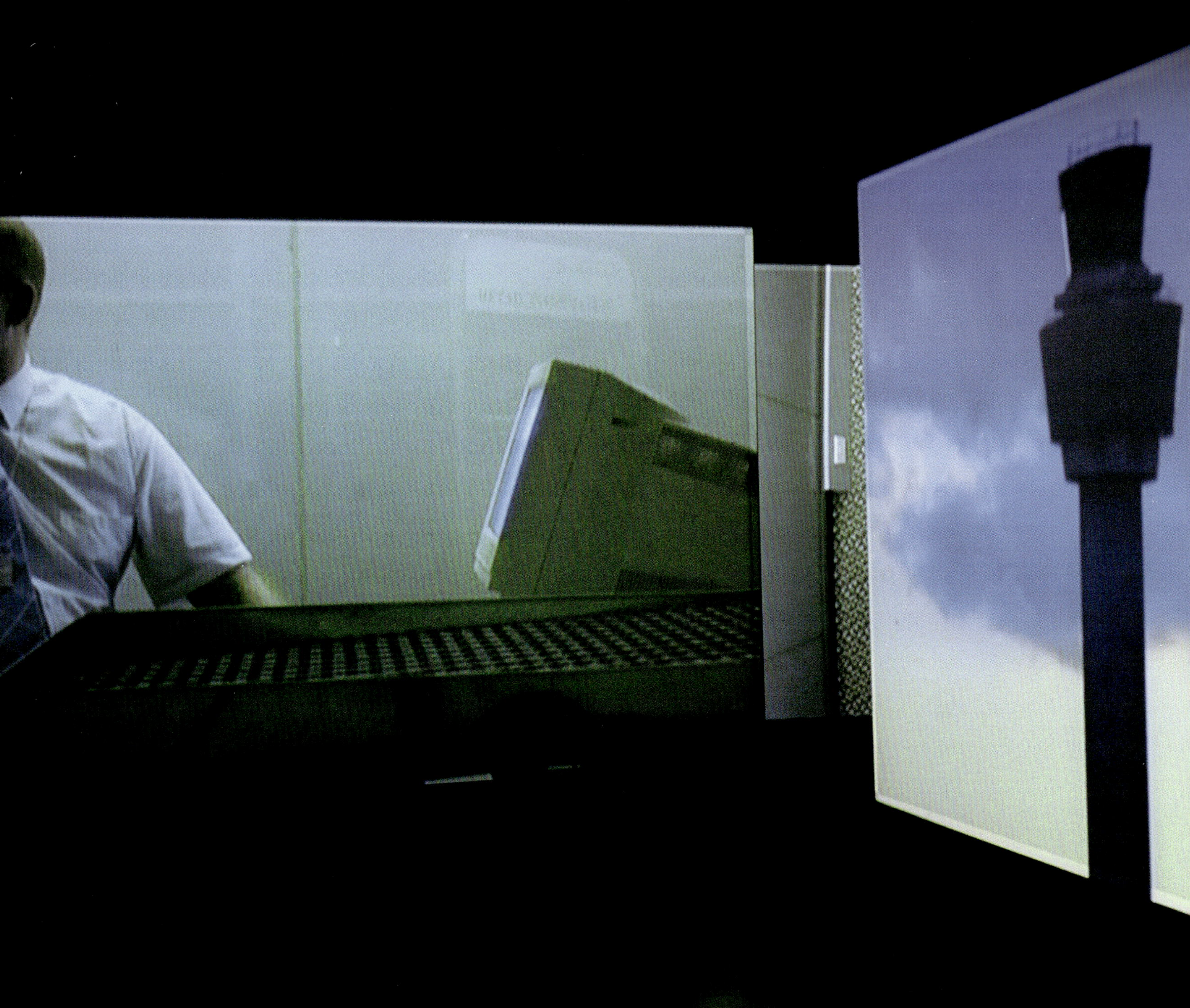

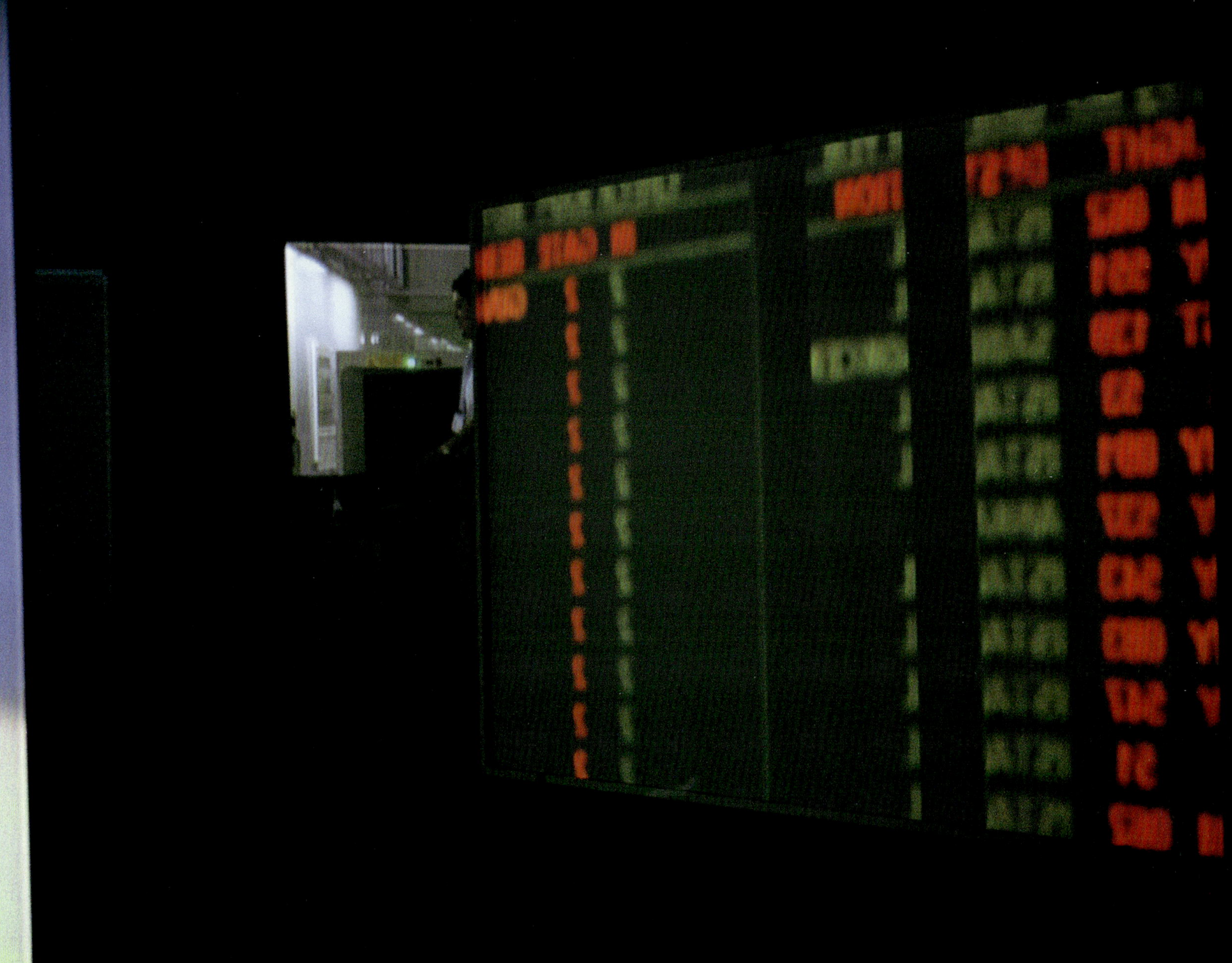

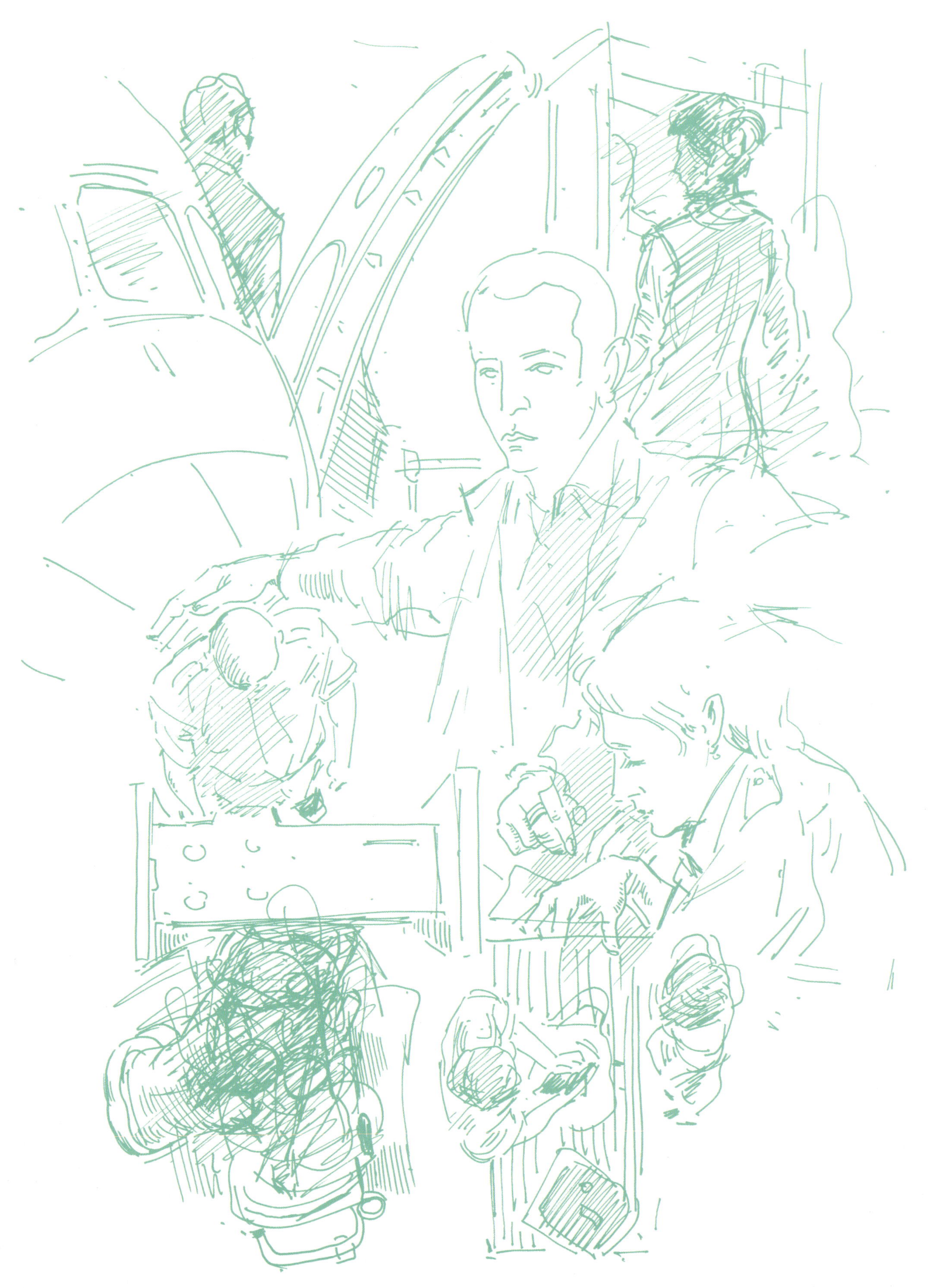

stansted–trabzon

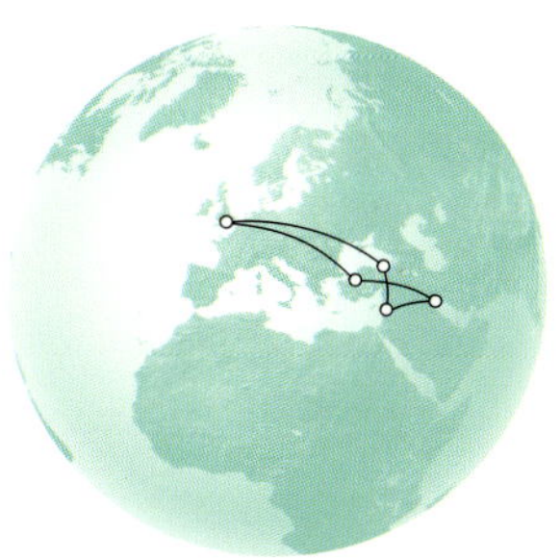

Itinerary

The Turkish Academic: Trabzon (TZX, 40° 55′N, 39° 50′E)–London Stansted (STN)–Points West *The English Journalist*: London Stansted (STN, 51° 53′N, 0° 14′E)–Damascus (DAM)–Baghdad (SDA)–Eastern Anatolia (ADA)–Home (51° 29′N, 0° 0′W)

History and Orientation

Trabzon is a trading city *par excellence*. Situated on what was once a northern offshoot of the Silk Road, it was immortalised in Rose Macaulay's classic 1956 travelogue *The Towers of Trebizond*. It was founded as a Milesian commercial colony in 756 BC and was later home to the Pontic Fleet, subsequently taken over by the Romans and renamed the *Classis Pontica*. Before the Romans the Greeks were here and after them the Goths. Today there are still sizeable Greek, Armenian, Abkhaz and Pontian Muslim populations in the city and it is still famous for its anchovies, hazelnuts and tea.

The **Airport**, 6km from the centre, was built in 1957, in a decorative modernist style. It buzzes with local colour and variety where more modern airports seem crowded into an orthodoxy of travelling fashion. Its rhythms are more of the market than the transport terminus. The terminal has high well-lit ceilings, a gallery, and elegant marble floors and columns which, on a fine day, warmly reflect the bright, if brooding, light of the Black Sea, a mere stone's throw away. All in all, a friendly and convivial place.

Much less well-known is **Stansted Mountfitchet**, the village after which the airport is named. It is another historical settlement, appearing in the Domesday book, but it is under the tourist radar that centres on the international airport.

Stansted Airport, built by architect Norman Foster, was hailed as an architectural masterpiece when it was opened in 1991, but now seems a little cluttered with retail and restaurant franchises. It has a 'floating' roof and was designed to allow single-level flow from car parks to terminal to departure, for the most part in natural light. Its predominant textures are stainless steel and grey and black carpet. The airport is efficient and polite in its processing of millions of budget travellers each year. It is designated to deal with any 'at-risk' flights approaching London and has facilities to keep hijackers well away from terminal and passengers.

Ancient Approaches

The Romans came and went in both Stansted and Trabzon. The Empire's roads ran all around the Essex countryside, coming close to what is now the airport through the ancient route between Great Dunmow and Takeley. At that time Hadrian was defining the antique version of what has recently been expressed by the artist Ergin Çavuşoğlu as 'the end points of the European idea'. New roads came through Trabzon and linked west and east over the Zigana Pass. Routes to and from Mesopotamia and Persia were opened up under Vespasian and Hadrian and the latter constructed a new harbour at the beginning of the second century AD. Stansted provided London with a new airport in 1991 and continues to open up newer cheaper routes. Here, during the 1985 expansion of the airport, two Roman burial sites were found at what became known as the 'in-flight catering site' (because of its then land-use), perhaps victims of Queen Boadicea's rebellious appetite. After the collapse of the USSR, Trabzon became a transit point in so called 'Natasha' trafficking, ensnaring girls from points east and north. Today it is a busy trading hub, most commodities slipping quietly through the glare of the Bosphorus…

Simon Harvey

Landscapes of Mobilities

Claire Doherty

Amongst the photographic souvenirs of my family's recent past is a rather odd portrait of my brother and me. We're dressed in our school uniforms and I must be about eight, which would make my brother eleven. We're resting on a luggage trolley which displays the notice 'London Heathrow' and we bear the world-weary expressions of passengers in transit. And yet we weren't travelling nor were we meeting anyone who was travelling.

This is a production still. We were extras on the set of the film *International Velvet*, a 70s sequel to the somewhat more memorable *National Velvet* with teenage diva Tatum O'Neal replacing Elizabeth Taylor as the equestrian heroine. The set was Stansted Airport, which in 1978 had yet to undergo Norman Foster's transformation. Its fate as London's third airport was announced the following year. I remember it as no more than an airfield bunker. Inside it had been dressed as Heathrow's International Terminal — the site of O'Neal's homecoming on winning her Olympic gold. In the late 70s, airports were still perceived as sites of privileged mobility, though the onset of low-cost travel had been signalled by the Laker Skytrain in 1977. The combination of film set and fictional jet-set led in this case to the pretence of privilege, though mobility was strangely impotent. The 'jet-setting' was practiced through a series of exits and entrances that led 'backstage', an endless cycle of identical welcomes and farewells, all for a cinematic fragment that lasted only 50 seconds in the final cut.

Stansted Airport in this photograph is not immediately recognisable as the place of Marc Augé's 'fleeting, temporary and ephemeral' encounters or Iain Chambers' "collective metaphor of cosmopolitan existence where the pleasure of travel is not only to arrive, but also not to be in any particular place." This was a particular place.[1] A materially evident place of intersections between real and imagined experiences and histories, political and economic relations, grounded in a mapped location, as Simon Harvey indicates elsewhere in this publication, 51˚53'N, 0˚14'E. This was, and was not, an airport. We were in, and out, of place.

Standing in Ergin Çavuşoğlu's complex and multi-layered representation of Stansted and Trabzon, I have the same sense of disorientation rooted in the materialities and characteristics of those airports. Some 28 years later, the Stansted of Çavuşoğlu's film still operates as a stage-set on which both spontaneous and scripted, real and imagined narratives are played out for the camera, and yet of course this Stansted is now the intersection of a new set of economic and political relations, with the aspirations of 70s air travel giving way to the anxiety of mobilities and migration in a post 9/11 world.

To associate Çavuşoğlu's mesmerising video installations merely with the conventions of non-place, and to view his work solely through the prism of migration between East and West, would be to miss his engagement with the details that make up specific places in space and time. Reviewers refer consistently to the poetic and lyrical qualities of his work and to his ability to transcend the documentary in favour of something less tangible, less illustrative. Çavuşoğlu's compositional approach suggests the artist is not interested in *replicating* the experience of the everyday, either as Michel de Certeau has discussed, from the totalising viewpoint of above, nor from the 'oblivion' of the street.[2] Rather, I believe him to be intrigued by the representation and remaking of place as understood by geographer Tim Cresswell as 'an event marked by openness and change rather than boundedness and permanence ... in a constant sense of becoming through practice and practical knowledge.'[3] To think about how and what these video installations signify about place, we need to begin by considering what we understand by the term 'place' itself.

In the 1970s, the work of human geographers such as Yi-Fu Tuan and Edward Relph posited a bounded notion of place, a moral converse to the rootlessness of mobility. Relph suggested:

> Roads, railways, airports, cutting across or imposed on the landscape rather than developing within it, are not only features of placelessness in their own right, but, by making possible the mass movement of people with all their fashions and habits, have encouraged the spread of placelessness well beyond their immediate impacts.[4]

This essentialist theorising of place, characterised as 'sedentarist metaphysics' by anthropologist Liisa Malkki, can be seen to have been destabilised through the postmodern philosophies of Gilles Deleuze and Felix Guattari and Michel Foucault in the 1980s and by cultural theorists such as James Clifford and Edward Said in the 1990s.[5] For Said, mobility and migration mark out the places of the modern age:

> For surely it is one of the unhappiest characteristics of the age to have produced more refugees, migrants, displaced persons, and exiles than ever before in history, most of them as an accompaniment to and ironically enough, as afterthoughts of great post-colonial and imperial conflicts. As the struggle for independence produced new states and new boundaries, it also produced homeless wanderers, nomads, vagrants, unassimilated to the emerging structures of institutional power, rejected by the established order for their intransigence and obdurate rebelliousness.[6]

And for Clifford:

> For better or worse, diaspora discourse is being widely appropriated. It is loose in the world, for reasons having to do with decolonization,

1 See Marc Augé, *Non-Places: Introduction to an Anthropology of Supermodernity*, trans. John Howe, London, Verso, 1995, and Iain Chambers, *Border Dialogues: Journeys in Postmodernity*, Routledge, London/New York, 1990, p.58.

2 Michel De Certeau, Ed. *The Practice of Everyday Life*, trans. Steven Rendall, University of California Press, Berkeley, 1984.

3 Tim Cresswell, 'Theorizing Place' in Tim Cresswell and Ginette Verstraete, Eds. *Mobilizing Place, Placing Mobility. The Politics of Representation in a Globalized World*, Amsterdam/New York, NY, 2002, pp.25–26.

4 Edward Relph qtd., in Tim Cresswell, *op.cit.*, p.14.

5 Liisa Malkki, 'National Geographic: The Rooting of Peoples and the Territorialization of National Identity Among Scholars and Refugees', *Cultural Anthropology*, 7th January 1992, pp.24–44.

6 Edward Said, *Culture and Imperialism*, Vintage, London, 1994, pp.402–403.

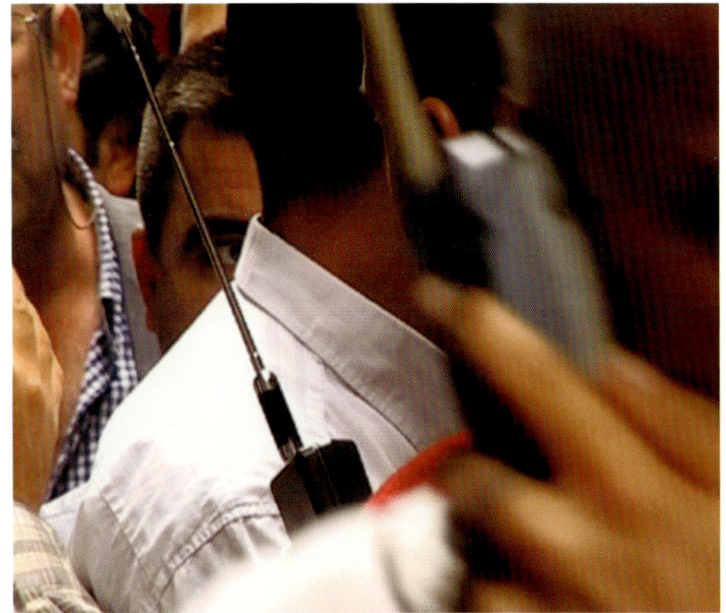

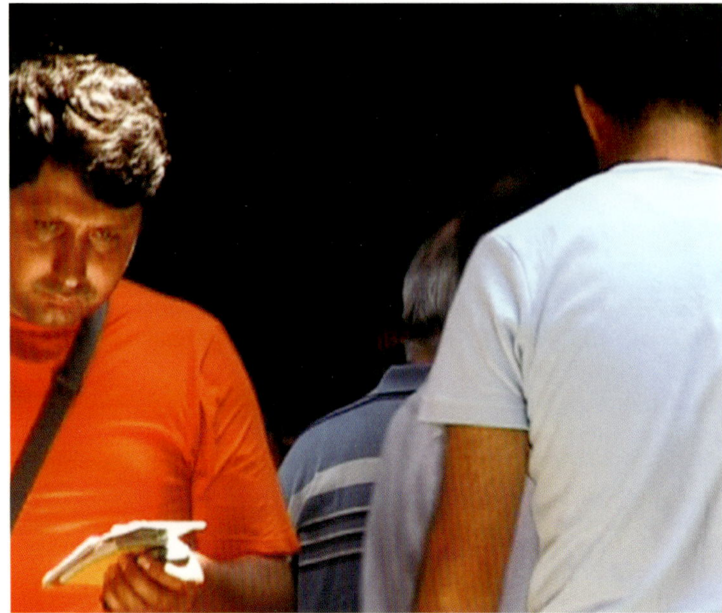

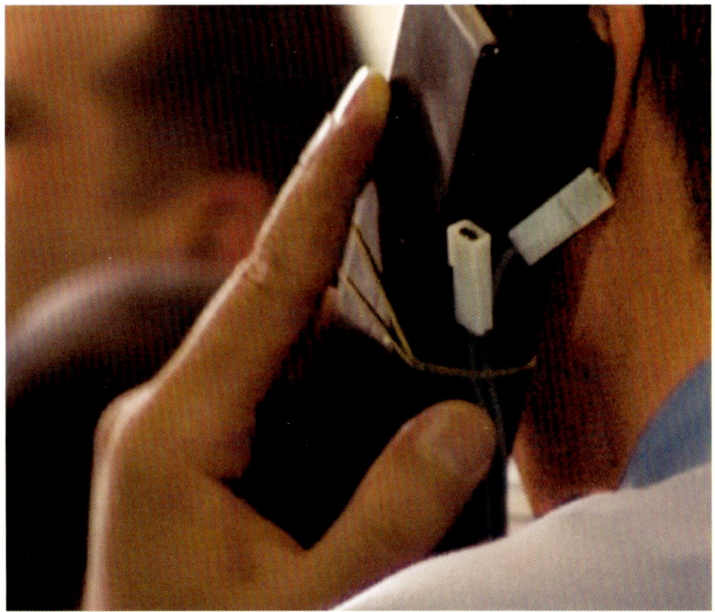

Is anybody selling exact?
I've got exact.
Abdullah Bey is leading the way.
Yes, Sir.
Shh, what happened?
Ismail what are you saying?
Buy for fifteen.
Hot, hot simiiit!
We are ready, buy for tomorrow.
I buy all sorts, all sorts, ready for 35.
Ready, ready buy for $35, ready for Thursday.
200 to 100. Hit the fucking thing.
Ridvan, how much is it?
My friend, go a bit this way.
Mr Hasan will buy all sorts.
Ready, it's 2 o'clock, 4, 5?

Tahtakale (2004)

> increased immigration, global communications, and transport — a whole range of phenomena that encourage multilocale attachments, dwelling, and traveling within and across nations.[7]

Forced and voluntary mobility was occurring in the postmodern world, by what David Harvey has referred to as unparalleled 'time-space compression' in light of the expansion of telecommunications and transport routes. The politics of mobilities and the diasporic condition came to dominate visual art and culture in the 1990s, yet, as Cresswell suggests, with the proliferation of 'nomadic metaphysics' came a "formalist, postmodern tendency to overgeneralize the global currency of the so-called nomadic, fragmented and deterritorialized subjectivity." The problem with mobility, Cresswell argues, is that it may serve to "decontexualise and flatten out difference as if we were all in fundamentally similar ways always already travellers in the same postmodern universe, the only difference residing in the different itineraries we undertake."[8]

So how do such nomadic metaphysics relate to Çavuşoğlu's work? By reading his landscapes of mobility and exchange (the port, the airport, the market, the station) simply as signifiers of the globalised flow of social relations, we are in danger of erasing their gendered, racial and social differences.[9] Essentially we may forget about the power relations that are brought to bear on these gateways that distinguish one passenger, worker, tourist and refugee from another. Let's take *Tahtakale* (2004) as an example.

This four-screen video installation presents a crowd of men trading in Istanbul's Grand Bazaar. An adjacent screen of scrolling text reports translated excerpts of their conversations on mobiles and cried out to each other. They are trading in currency and gold. The atmosphere is frenzied, yet informal. *Tahtakale* is distinguished from Çavuşoğlu's other recent work by its intensity of focus and energy. There are no establishing panoramic or tracking shots here, but rather the artist embeds his camera in the crowd. It is here in Tahtakale that Turkish fiscal policy is set, economic relations are played out through the haggling techniques of the market. We could read *Tahtakale* as the representation of an historic site-specific practice which imbues the Grand Bazaar with its sense of the local. Or we could see the proliferation of mobile phones, the absence of traded objects and the westernised clothes of the traders as indications of Tahtakale as a deterritorialised zone. But of course the work is intent on the collision of both essentialised place and globalisation (particularly through the soundtrack with the combination of Byzantine male choir and animated transactions in dollars). This work offers us a more progressive notion of place — one that is gendered (the artist intentionally immerses the viewer in the machismo of the transactions), practiced and performed (Tahtakale only occurs through the intersections of specific social and economic relations) and defined by conflict. Tahtakale is the 'event in progress' theorised by geographer Doreen Massey in a ground-breaking article first published in 1993. Massey proposed that "what gives a place its specificity is not some long internalized history but the fact that it is constructed out of a particular constellation of relations."[10] We see this response to place develop through Çavuşoğlu's recent multi-screen installations structurally, formally and conceptually.

The artist is still intrigued by the liminal spaces of the city that formed the subjects of his earlier single-screen works *Impasse*, *Street Dance* and *Mountain Bike*. Yet his use of multiple large-scale projections now fractures the single-point perspective, so that the installations envelop the viewer. This formal structure serves to heighten a sense of spatial displacement, but also alludes to the cinematic — whereby the projections act as split screens in a narrative from multiple perspectives.

Poised in the Infinite Ocean (2004) and *Downward Straits* (2004) utilise this formal structure to exploit the darkness across the screens. Architectural details are obscured, recognisable figures are absent, ships become shadows and the blackness of the water is set against the illumination of the buildings. In *Downward Straits* in particular, Hagia Sofia, Ortaköy Mosque and Kuleli Barracks (the institutions of church and the military) provide a static backdrop to the automated movement. The staccato wireless radio broadcasts and lapping waves cut into the solitude of the vistas set up between the screens. Michel Foucault famously declared:

> ... the boat is a floating piece of space, a place without a place, that exists by itself, that is closed in on itself and at the same time is given over to the infinity of the sea and that from port to port, from tack to tack, from brothel to brothel, it goes as far as the colonies in search, of the most precious treasures they conceal in their gardens, you will understand why the boat has not only been for our civilisation..., the greatest instrument of economic development... but has been simultaneously the greatest reserve of the imagination. The ship, is the heterotopia par excellence.[11]

The narration of *Poised in the Infinite Ocean* captures this somewhat romantic notion of the ship as heterotopia, whilst the illuminated buildings act as anchor points or nodes in the networks of movements through the Bay of Biscay. Çavuşoğlu experiments with darkness in both of these installations to shift the subject from the specifics of locations to their imaginative potential. The narrative cohesion of *Poised in the Infinite Ocean* gives way in *Adrift* (2006) and *Point of Departure* (2006) to a more complex multi-layering of time, mobilities and locations.

7 James Clifford, *The Predicament of Culture: Twentieth Century Ethnography, Literature and Art*, Harvard U P, 1988, p.249. See also James Clifford, *Routes: Travel and Translation in the Late Twentieth Century*, Harvard University Press, Cambridge, 1997.

8 Tim Cresswell, *op.cit.*

9 Tim Cresswell, 'The Production of Mobilities', *New Formations 43*, 2001, p.17.

10 Doreen Massey, 'Power-Geometry and a Progressive Sense of Place', in J. Bird, et al. Eds. *Mapping the Futures*, Routledge, London, 1993.

11 Michel Foucault, 'Of Other Spaces', 1967, published in *Architecture/Mouvement/ Continuité*, October, 1984. http://roundtable.kein.org/node/119 (7th May 2006).

Adrift moves away from allusions to film noir towards observational montage which nevertheless still retains a certain unease. As far as I can tell there is no significant connection between Çavuşoğlu's choice of locations here — Centraal Station in Antwerp and Carnegie Hall in New York, along with the outer neighbourhoods of the cities and Rhode Island. But the lack of a distinct narrative is important. The artist sets up a series of vignettes: the view of the skyline out of the train windows bumps and flickers with the movement of the carriage; the scale of people shifts from the miniature static figures of the architect's model to the on-lookers who simultaneously move around and within Louis Delacenserie's Centraal Station; a man in a yellow souwester jet-sprays the spindles of an external staircase inch-by-inch; gated mansions roll past echoing the architectural model; a disenfranchised figure sits by the roadside; a boy 'monkey-swings' on the scaffolding built around Carnegie Hall; stop-don't-walk signs blink; a Buddha shines through an illuminated doorway; a shaky camcorder captures a descending jet plane. These are the connections Çavuşoğlu makes for us between the performing of place in these locations. It is impossible to see these representations without thinking about how the spaces of the city and its environs are coded; how and where transgressions and interventions occur. And how the artist lets us see these spaces at one remove. The camera angles in *Adrift* are notable — the interchange from a window across the street, the skyline from inside a moving train, the sea from a boat. Çavuşoğlu positions us as passengers afforded glimpses of these 'events in progress'. As Massey suggests:

> People's routes through the place, their favourite haunts within it, the connections they make (physically, or by phone or post, or in memory and imagination) between here and the rest of the world vary enormously. If it is now recognised that people have multiple identities then the same point can be made in relation to places. Moreover, such multiple identities can either be a source of richness or a source of conflict, or both.[12]

It's the artist's astute use of two musical notes in the score for *Adrift* that, when repeated consistently for the entire duration of the work, creates that sense of unease. The inherent suspense of the discordant combination becomes increasingly unbearable as the notes never reach their final resolution. Combine that base tone with alarm bells and the movement of trains back and forth and you have a piece which relishes its uneasy indeterminate state — an aural and filmic *transito*.[13]

Çavuşoğlu is not interested in private, domesticated spaces, but rather in the intimate moments which lay claim to public space. The landscapes of mobility (the roads, railways, airports of Edward Relph's placelessness) are public and somewhat anonymous. For Çavuşoğlu, these spaces offer the opportunity to think about how identities are constructed through social and material interactions for people and for places and how in turn these might affect the viewer in other spaces.

Point of Departure (2006) is an ambitious development of these observational tendencies which coalesce to form a dialogue between the generic materials, rhythms and patterns of activity of Stansted and Trabzon Airports. At over 31 minutes, the piece can afford to linger, the static and tracking shots forming a kind of choreography of bodies and objects ambling across each screen. Çavuşoğlu has always been interested in the conjunction of darkness and colour, and here luminous scrolling x-rays and colourful, well-lit protagonists are played off against the dull tones of the mundane security activities.

Tim Cresswell asserts that "ironically, while the concept of routes is supposed to make connections and link people across borders, travel itself has often been driven by the desire to construct and consume difference."[14] Less 'uneasy' than *Adrift*, *Point of Departure* seems to be entirely caught up with the construction and consumption of difference. This is not a work about the methods of movement, though of course it is concerned with the politics and production of mobilities, nor is it concerned with 'placelessness' versus 'destination'. Rather, it seems to me to be about the intersection and collisions of multiple experiences of place. The Turkish traveller moves through a set of encounters which are coded, performed and surveyed, yet crucially his 'mobility' or capacity to move is differentiated from those around him. The security staff, pilots, local residents and other international travellers are all implicated in the power relations of the two airports. What *Point of Departure* leaves us with, through its complex structuring of viewpoints and perspectives, languages and silences, is Massey's extrovert sense of place. We can recognise some of the historical specificities of the places, whilst also seeing how players interact within these specified structures, how in effect place is produced in context.

Çavuşoğlu recognises the capacity of these intersecting points to reflect upon the contradictions of the postmodern world: one in which trading occurs in a gendered, historicised space; where the experience of European and North American cities is determined by cinematic and televisual representation; and where the place of the airport is charged with the thrill of new beginnings and encounters, but still remains resolutely a fiction of border crossings — an event which is both in and out of place.

12 Doreen Massey, *op.cit.*

13 An Italian word "untranslatable in English in one word," explains Giuliana Bruno; "a notion of circulation, including passages, traversals, transitions and transitory states." Giuliana Bruno, 'City Views: The Voyage of Film Images' in David B. Clarke, *The Cinematic City*, Routledge, London, 1997, p.46.

14 Tim Cresswell, 2002, p.27.

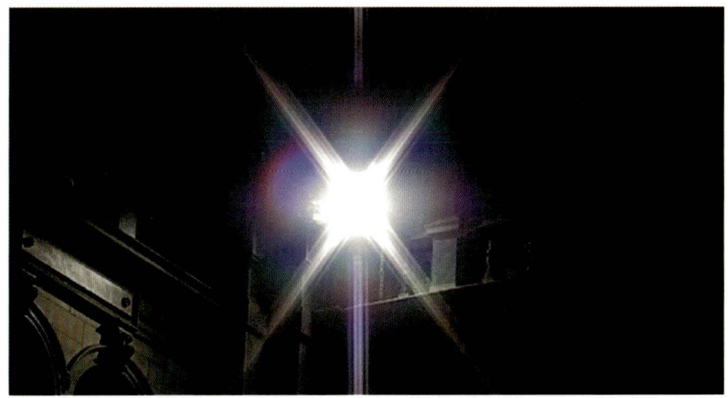

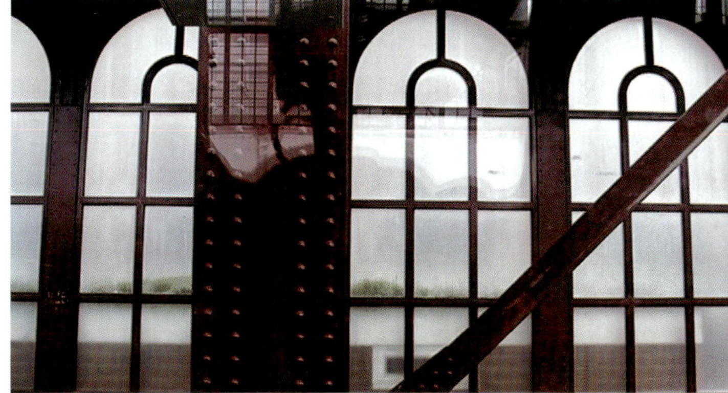

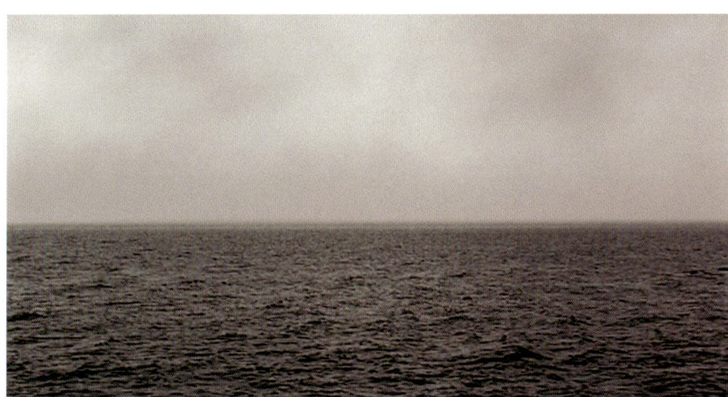

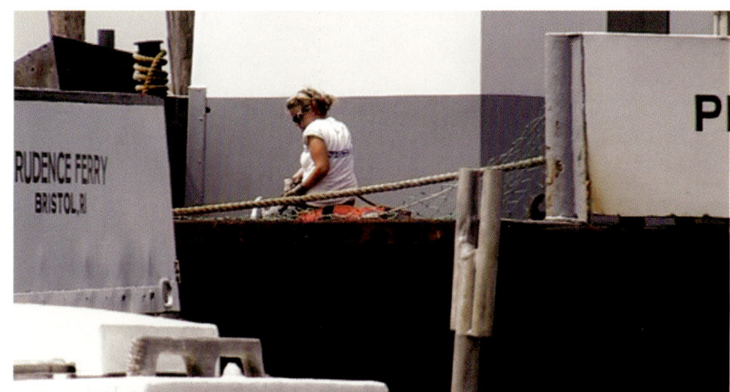

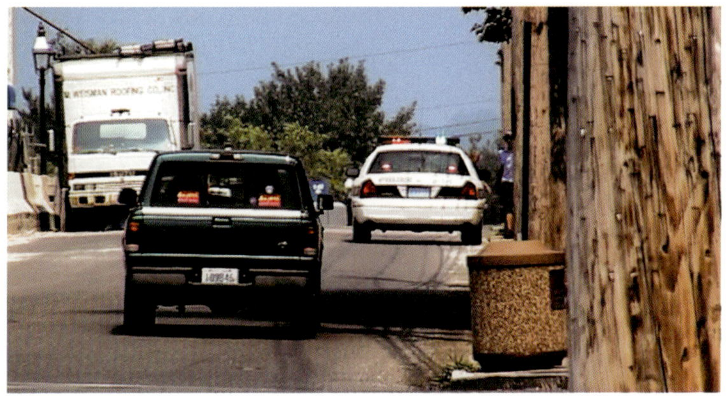

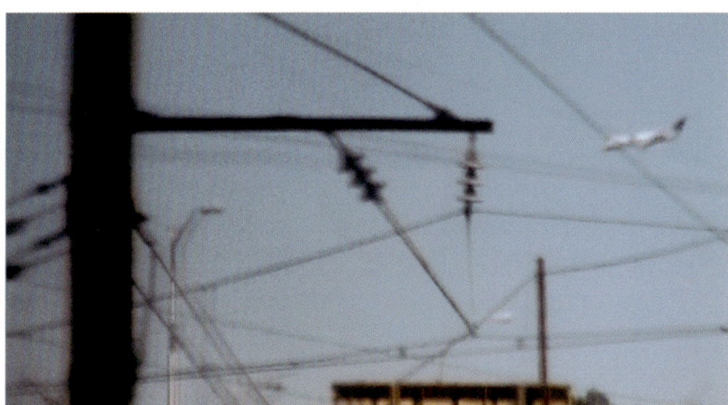

Adrift (2004)

Poised in the Infinite Ocean

Poised in the Infinite Ocean (2004)
Three-screen video installation, two channels sound
Reading from the book *The Outlaw Sea* by the author William Langewiesche
Running time: 05:20min, continuous loop
Dimensions variable: front/rear projection screens
Installation view: Manchester Art Gallery, 2006

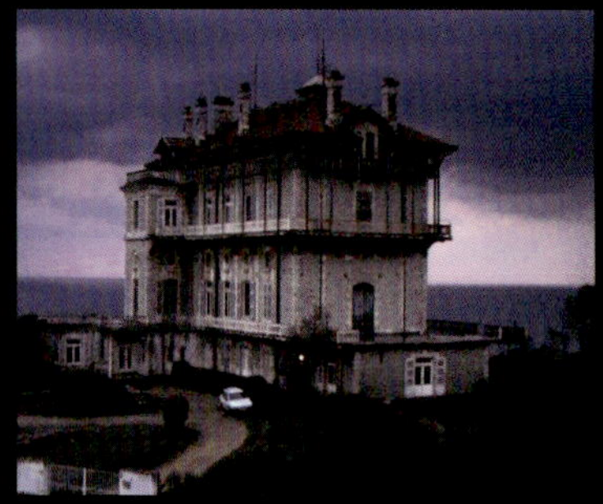

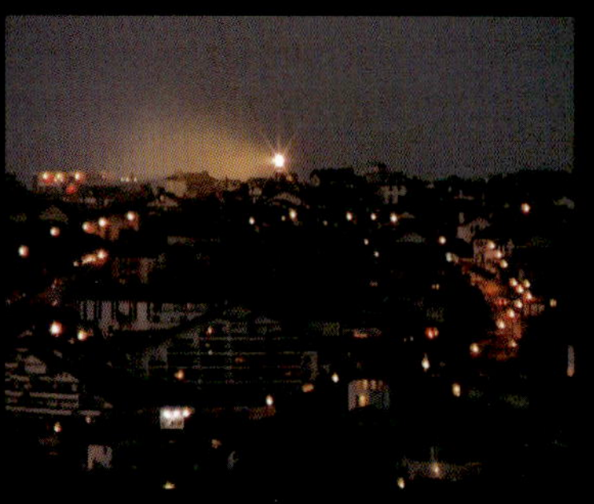
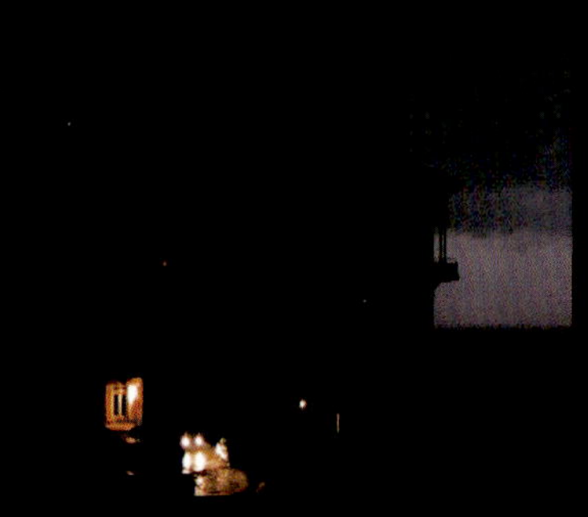
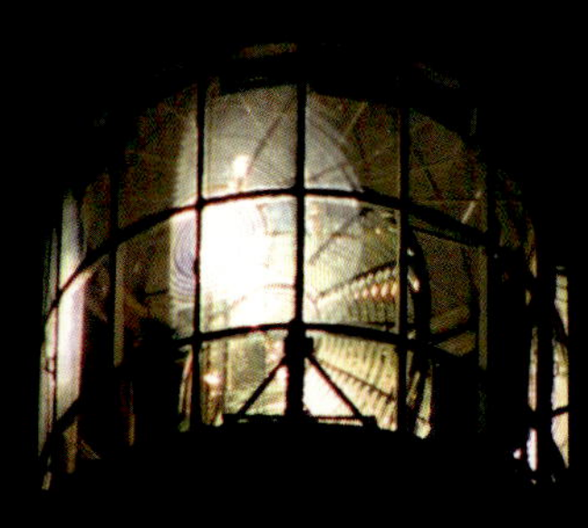
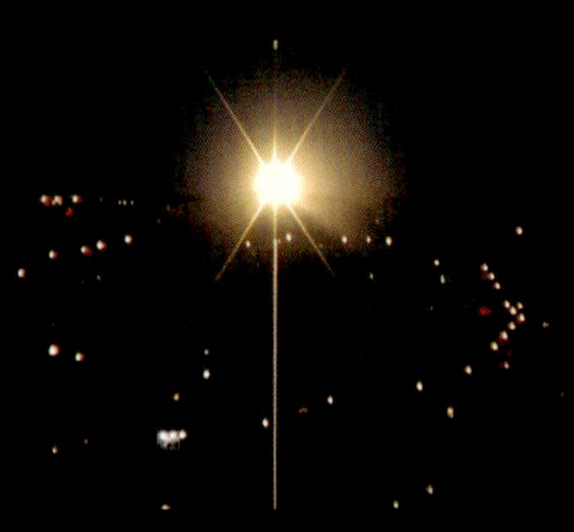
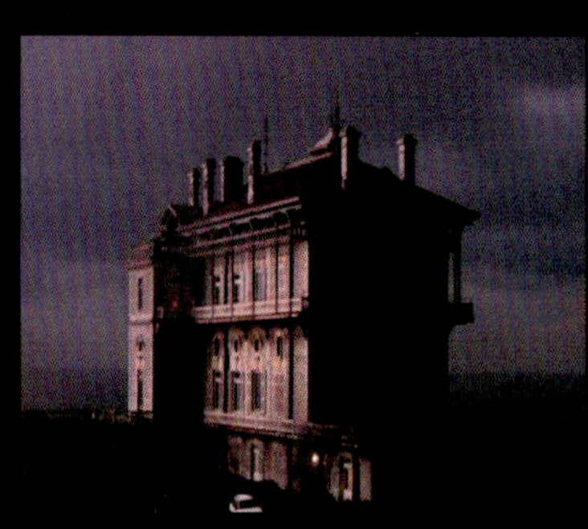
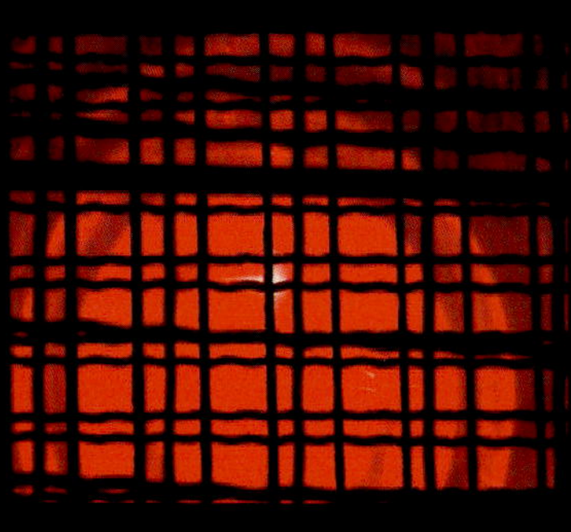
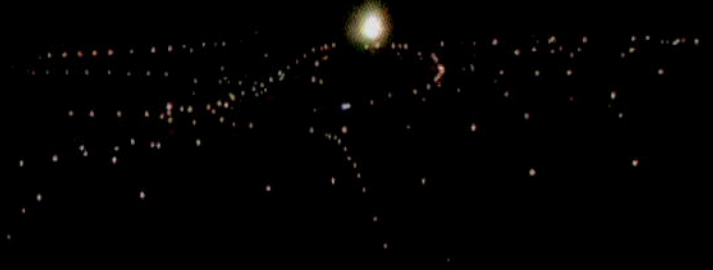

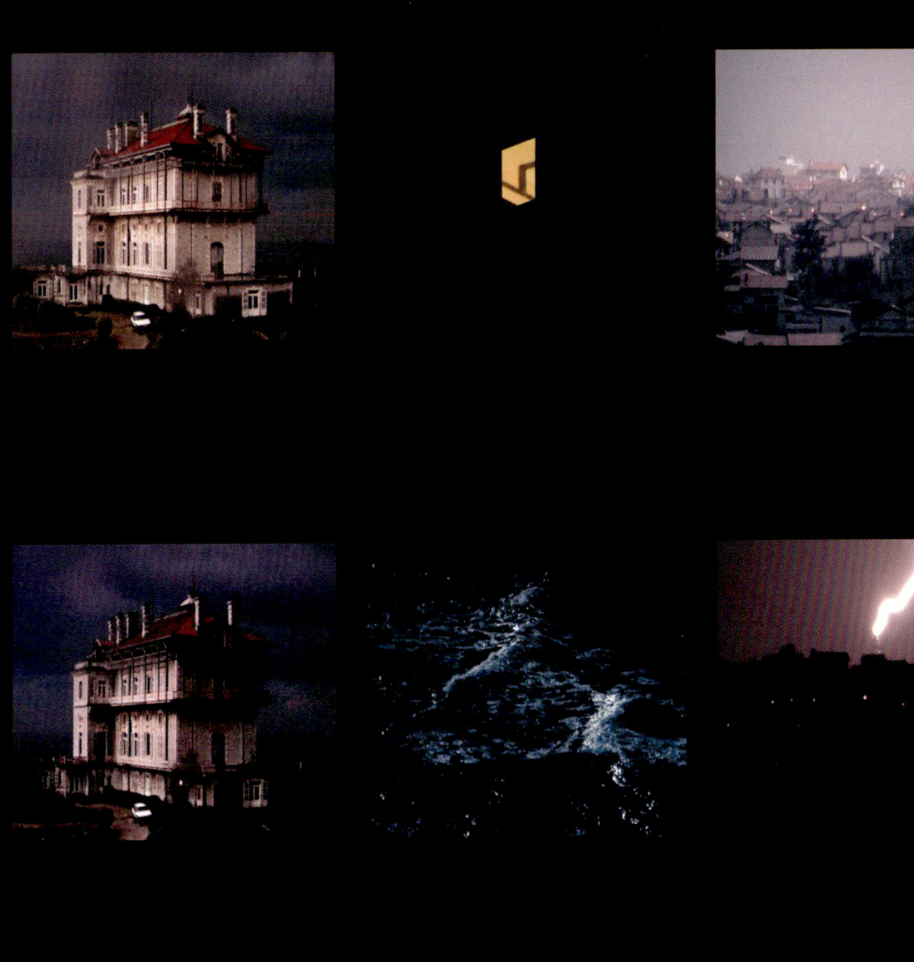
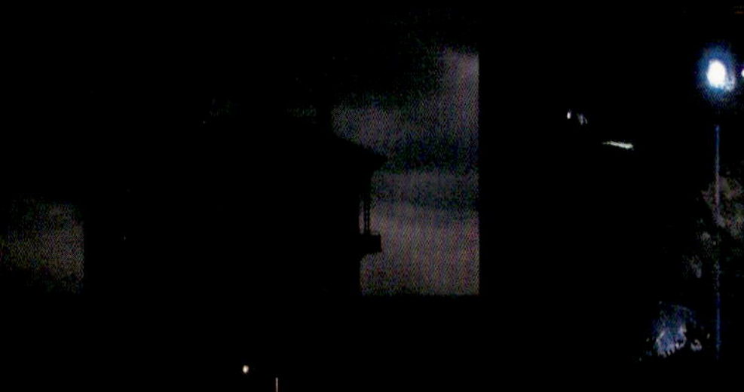
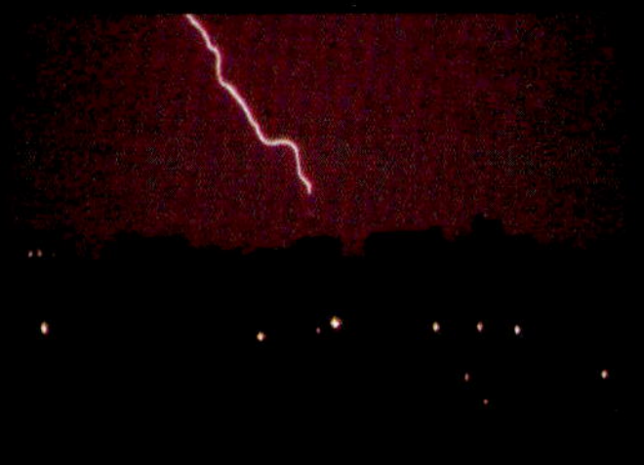

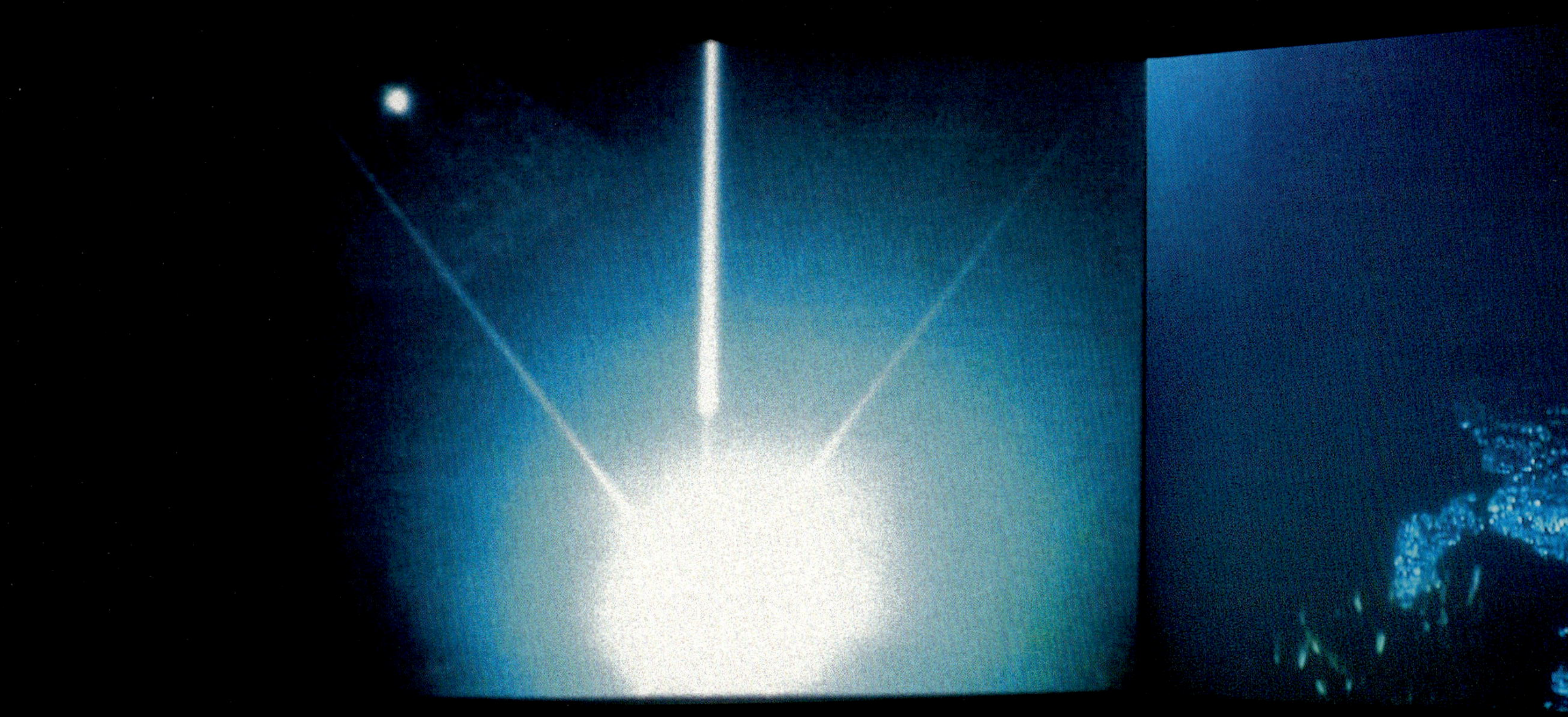

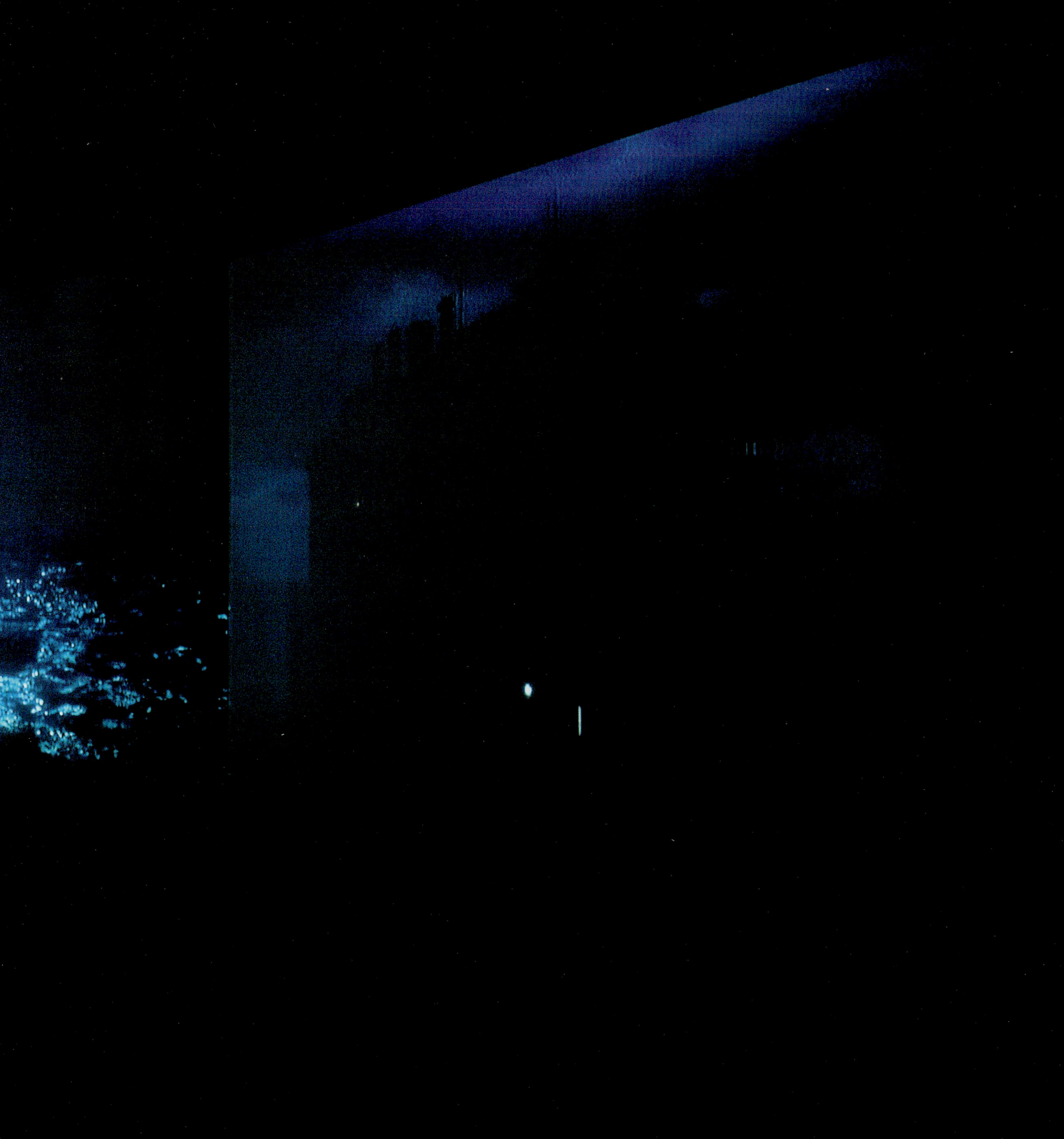

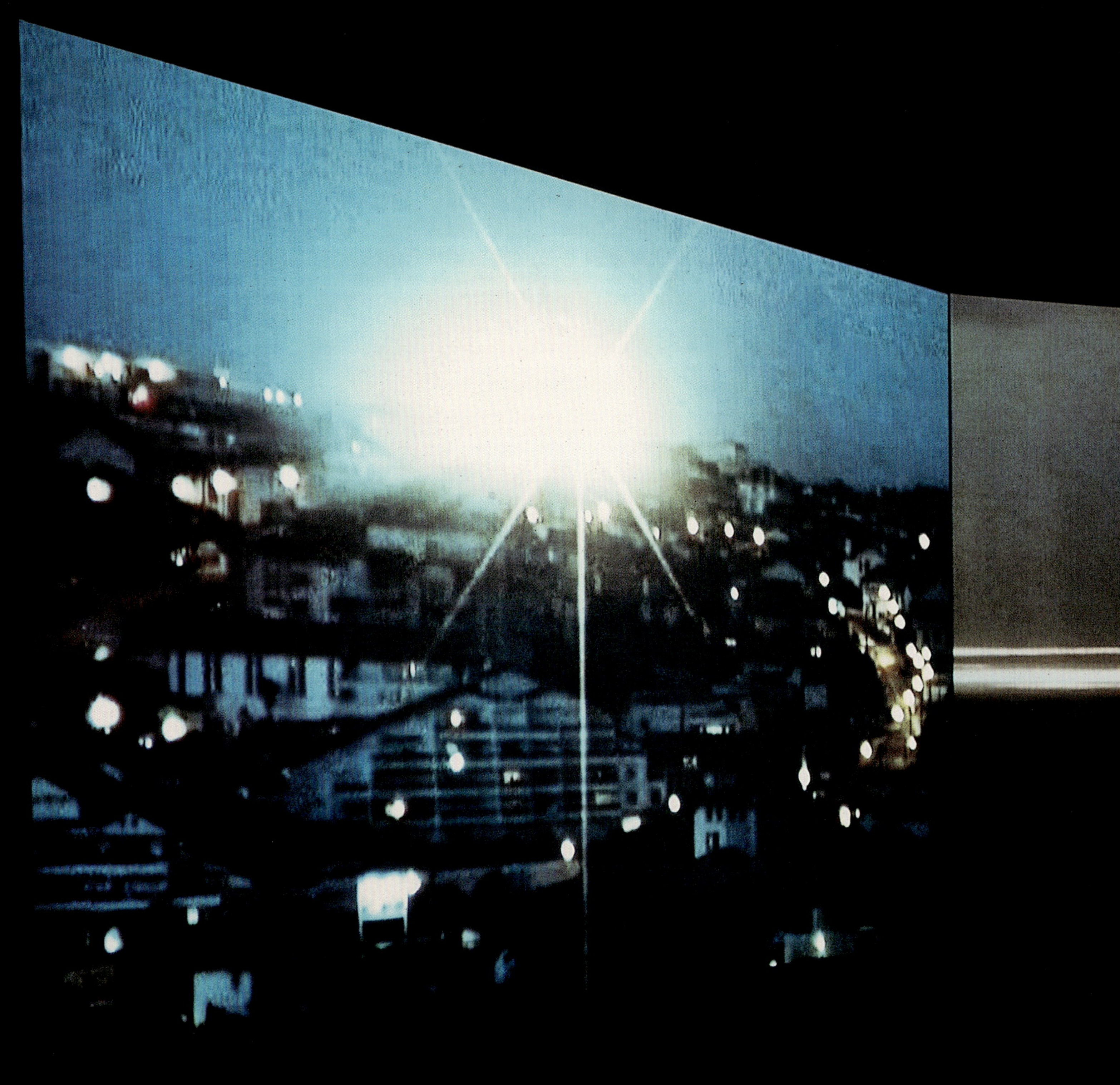

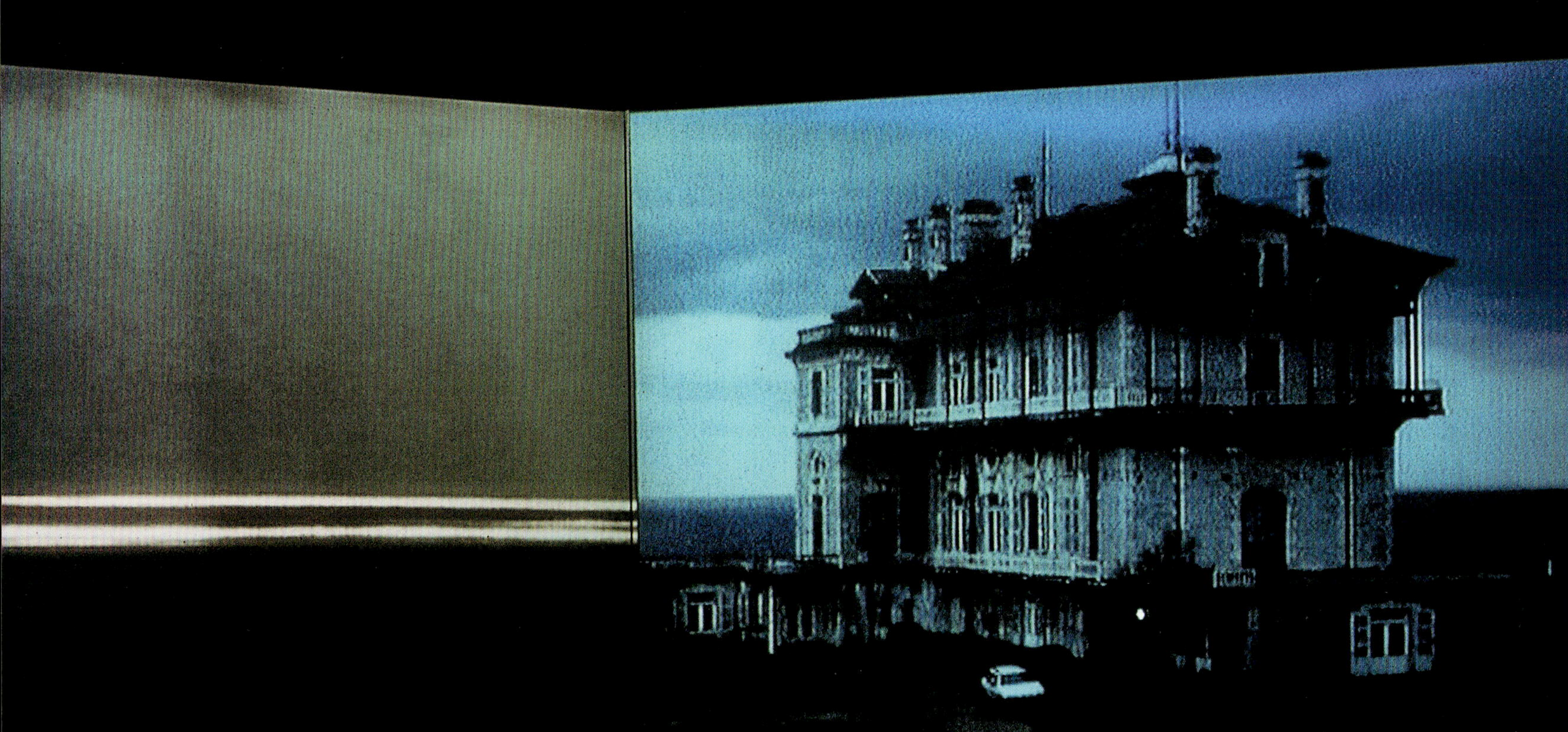

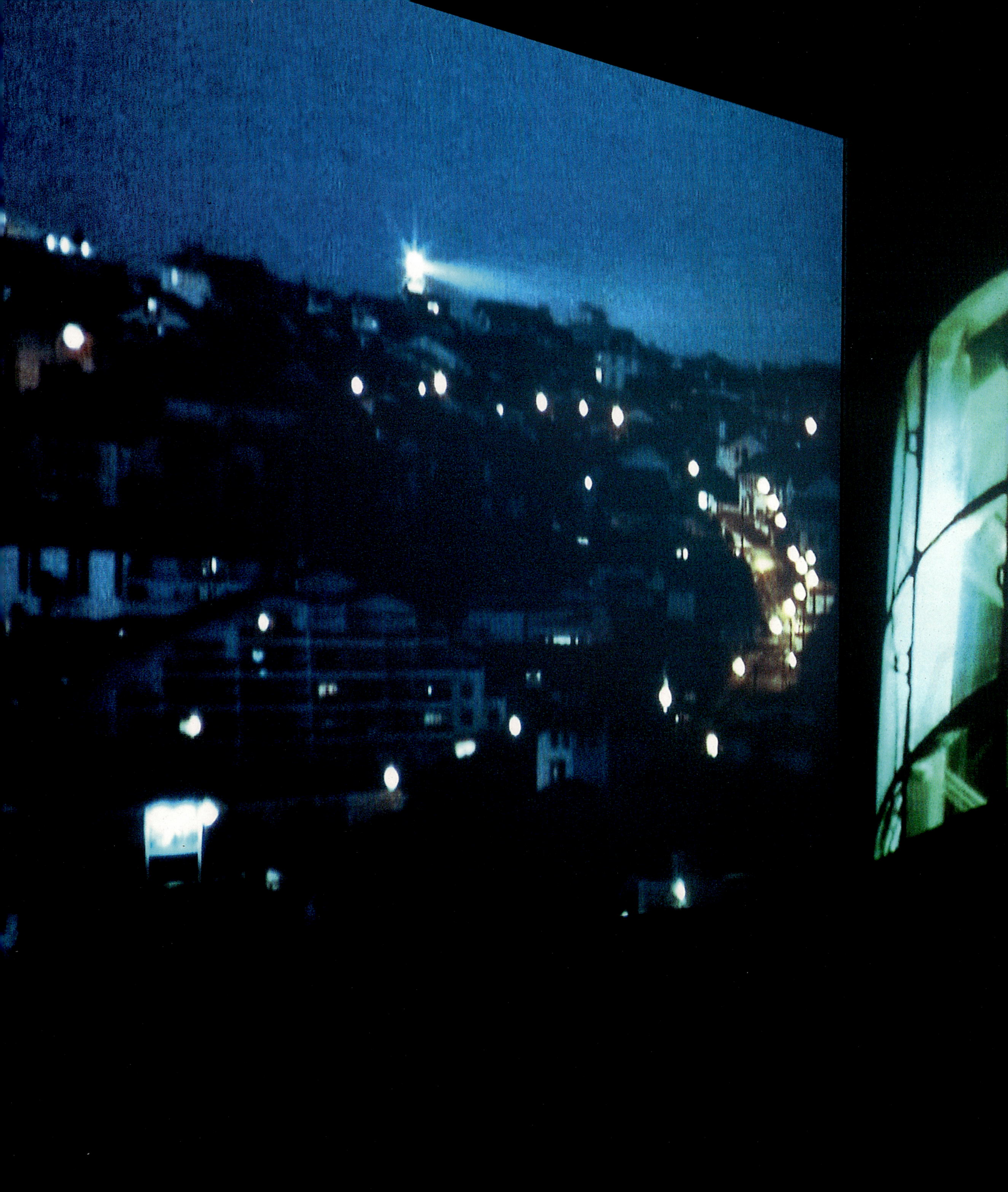

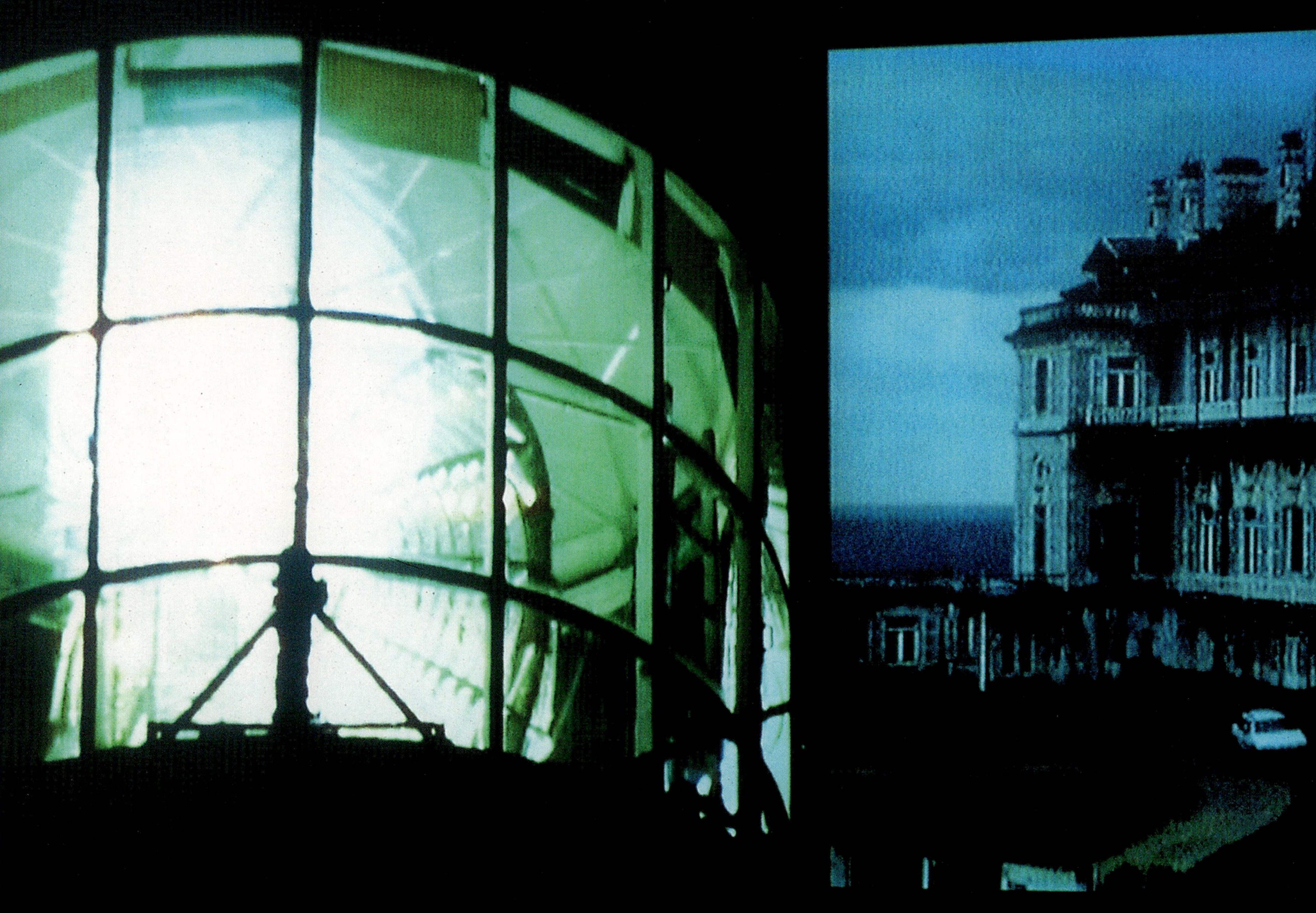

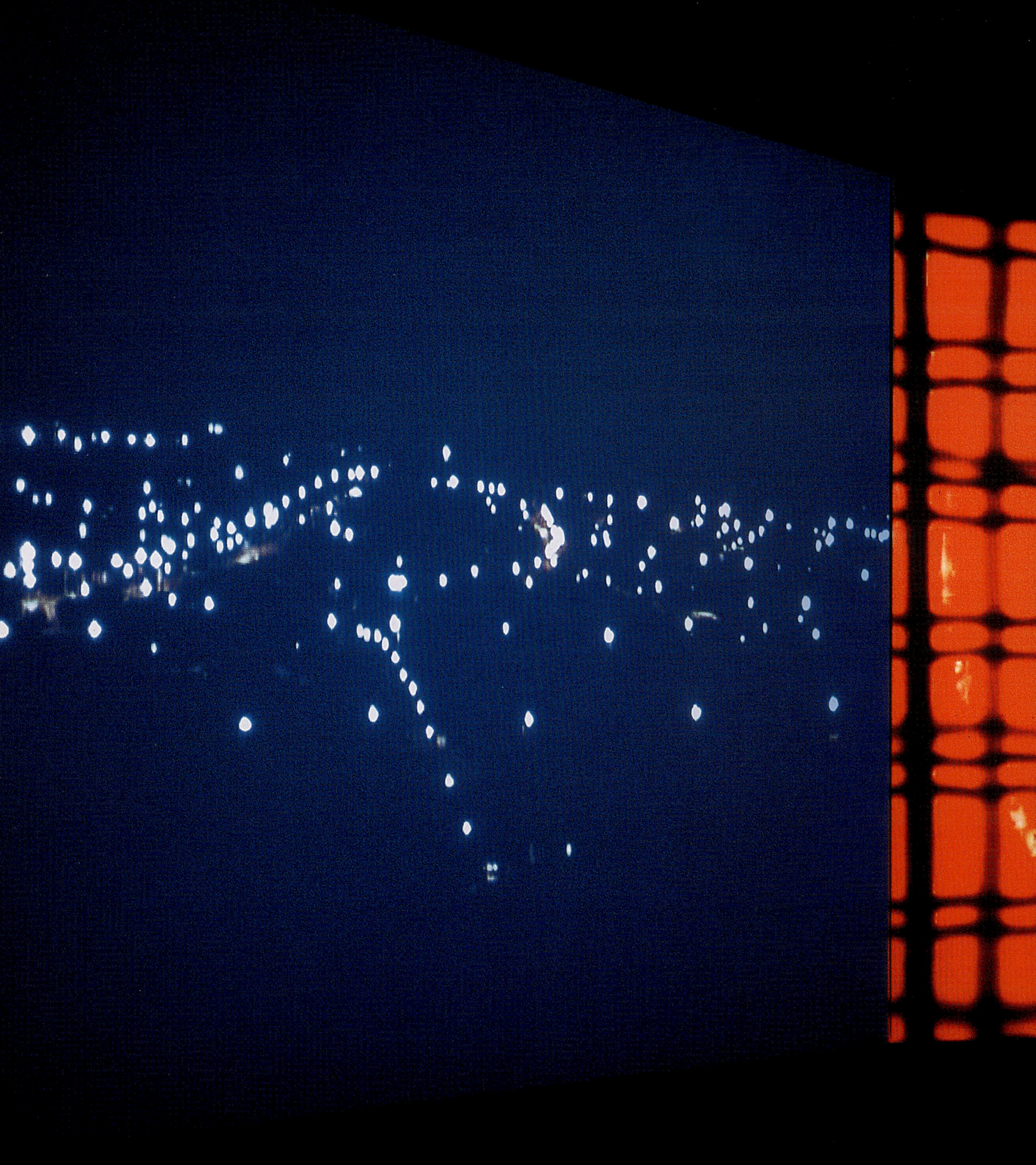

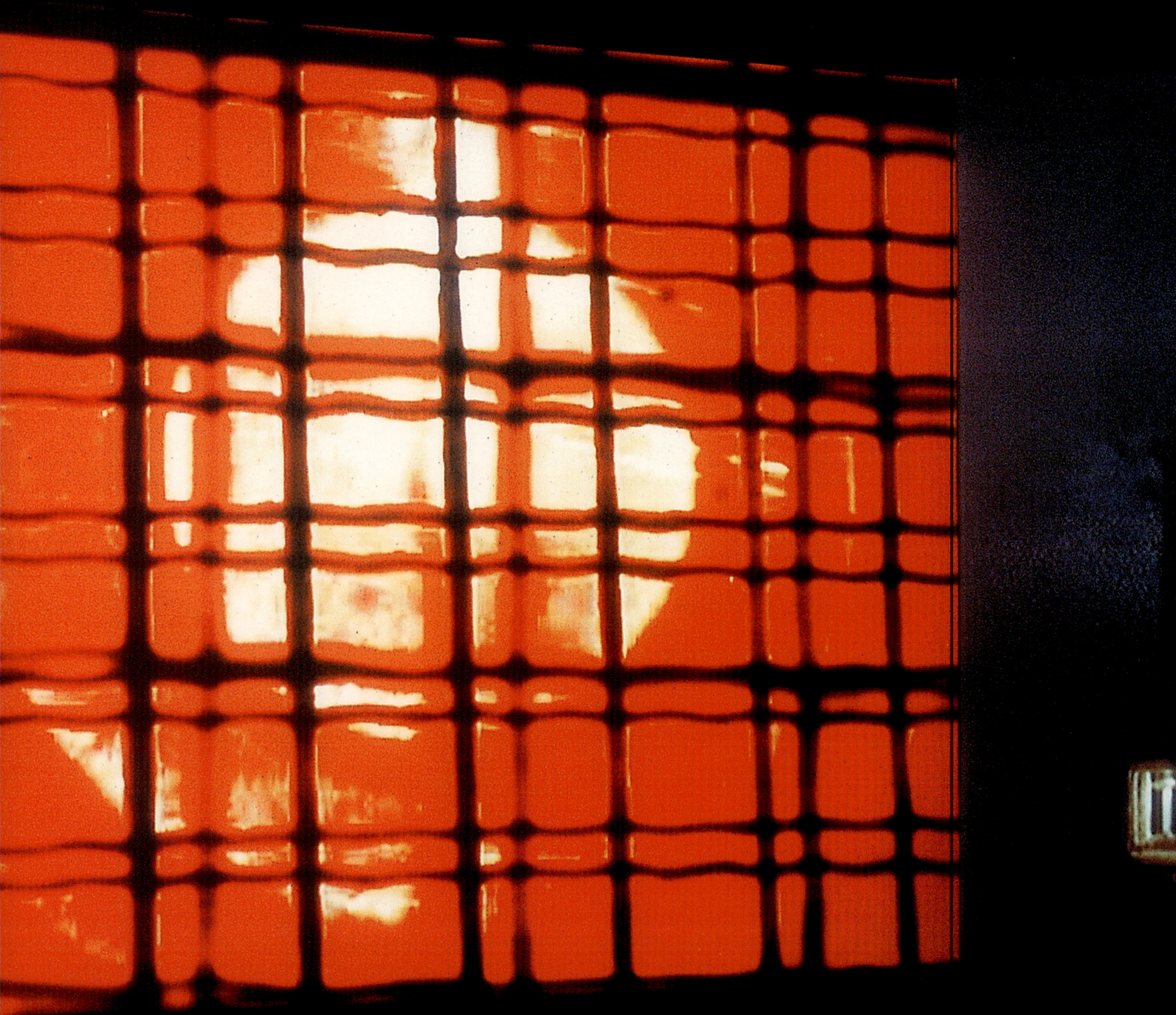

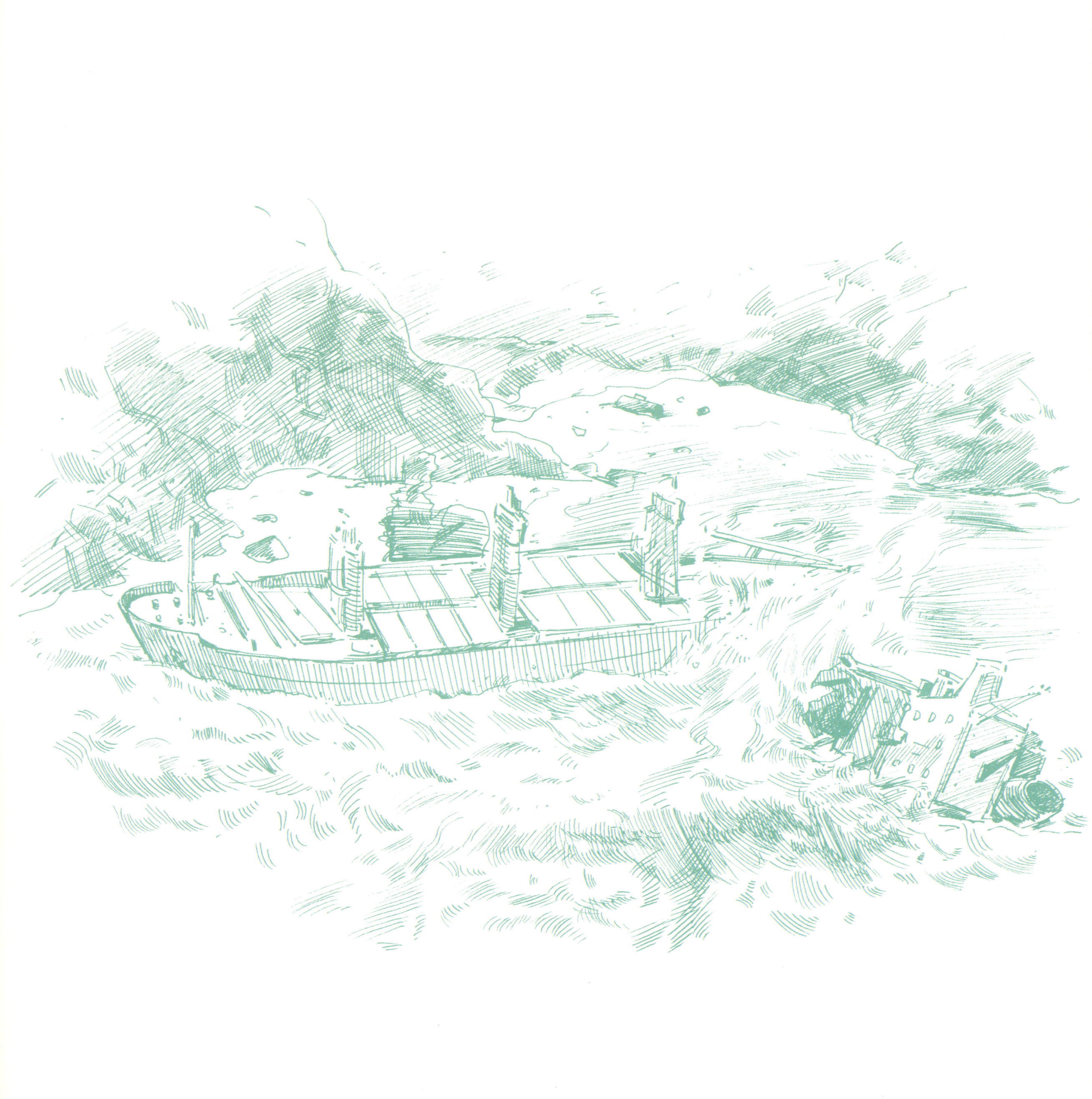

biscay

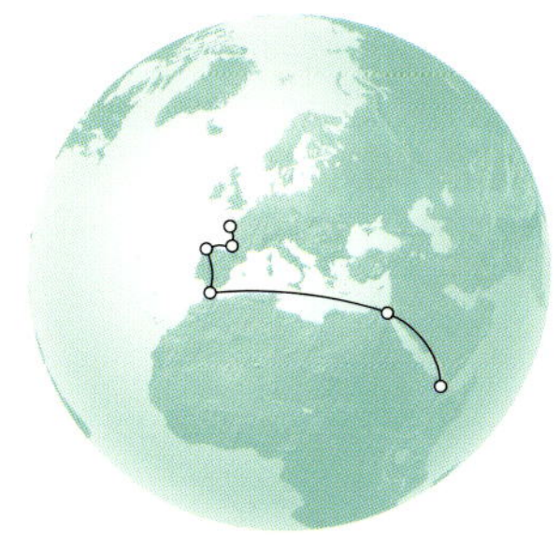

Itinerary

Points South–Bab al-Mandab (10° 28′N, 40° 37′E)–Suez (30° 0′N, 32° 35′E)–Straits of Gibraltar (36° 9′N, 5° 22′W)–Costa del Morte (Fitzroy)–Bay of Biscay–Cote Sauvage (Bidart, 43° 25′N, 1° 36′W)–Points North

Southern Approaches

The lighthouse at St Jean de Luz is a waymark on the Spice route that enters the Mediterranean at Suez, leaves it at the straits of Gibraltar and passes La Costa da Morte, Spain's wild Atlantic coastline around Coruña. In weather terms this is 'Fitzroy', formerly known as 'Finisterre', named after the father of shipping forecasts Admiral Robert Fitzroy, better known as the captain of HMS *Beagle*, conveyor of Darwin to the Galapagos. From here ships sail into the notorious Bay of Biscay, with its treacherous Côte Sauvage, before heading up to the markets of England, Holland, Belgium, Germany and points north. The brilliant red of the light continues to this day to cast a romantic, some say dangerous and melancholy, spell over the French Basque shoreline, serving as much as a reminder of spills and wrecks as a saviour of mariners.

The Basque Coast

At the southern end of France's western shore is the Côte Basque characterised by isolated lights and singular monuments presiding over ancient fishing ports punctuating long stretches of golden beach. Between St Jean de Luz and glitzy Biarritz there are a number of landmarks familiar and comforting to passing ships. The historic lighthouse at St Jean gives way to the imposing Chateau d'llbaritz at Bidart, while the Phare de Biarritz competes with the grand Hotel du Palais dominating its Promenade.

Biarritz

Biarritz is the centre for the region and came to prominence as a glamorous resort for European royalty and the rich and famous during the late nineteenth and early twentieth Centuries. In 1854 Empress Eugenie, wife of Napoleon III, built a palace here that was to become the **Hotel du Palais**, one of France's ritziest hotels. Originally a Nordic outpost and whaling centre, Biarritz's links with the sea are still strong. The Museum of the Sea has 24 aquarium tanks and brings much of the marine life of the Bay of Biscay within reach. For horizon gazers a must is the Phare de Biarritz on the cliffs above the town at the end of Rue de Sémaphore off Rue de Phare.

Bidart

The pretty Basque seafaring village of Bidart is nowadays almost a satellite of Biarritz. It has little of the latter's *fin de siècle* style but is nevertheless a popular beach destination for French holidaymakers, and attracts some of the international surfing crowd. It is dominated by the Chateau d'llbaritz, built in 1894 for the Baron Albert de L'Espee. It is on the threshold of Biarritz but looms forebodingly over the village. Even before its transformation into a headquarters for Nazi forces in the 1940s the Baron had brought Teutonic overtones to the municipality indulging his obsession for organ music in this 'House for Wagner'. On La Pointe St-Martin, the famous lighthouse signals the safe passage of shipping along this stretch of beautiful but tempestuous coastline.

St Jean de Luz

An ancient Basque port that has nevertheless become one of the newer resorts along this rugged shore. It is particularly noted for its seafood and is the centre of French Basque gastronomy. The outstanding building in the town is the Maison Louis XIV where the French king stayed before marrying Maria Theresa of Spain. This most Basque of towns was therefore the site of a broad imperial alliance when on June 6th 1660 Louis XIV signed the Treaty of the Pyrenees and three days later married in the Eglise St Jean-Baptiste, one of the finest churches in this part of France.

Simon Harvey

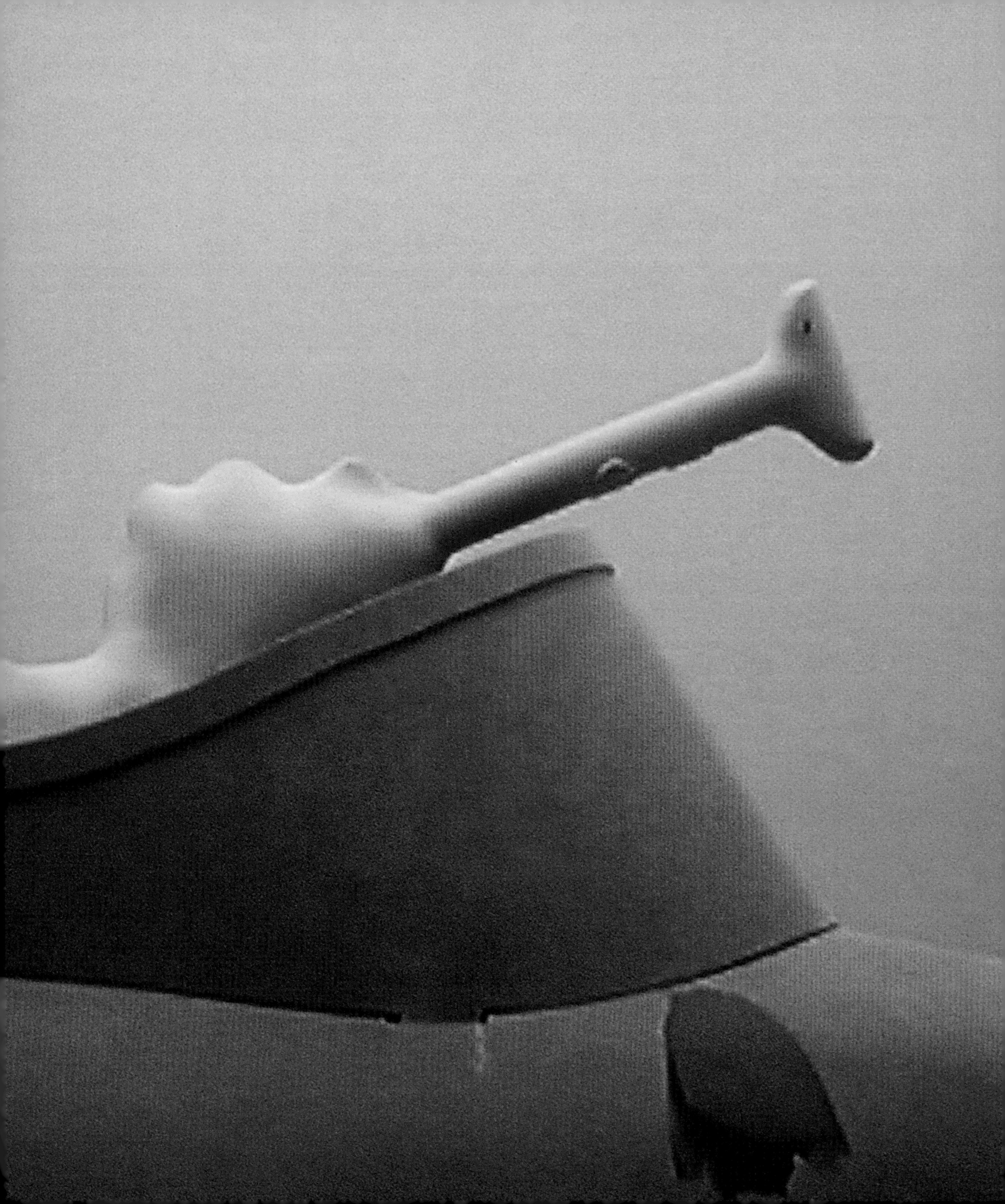

Adrift

Adrift (2006)
Four-screen video installation, sound
Running time: 06:01min, continuous loop
Dimensions variable: front/rear projection screens
Installation view: Northern Gallery for Contemporary Art, Sunderland, 2006

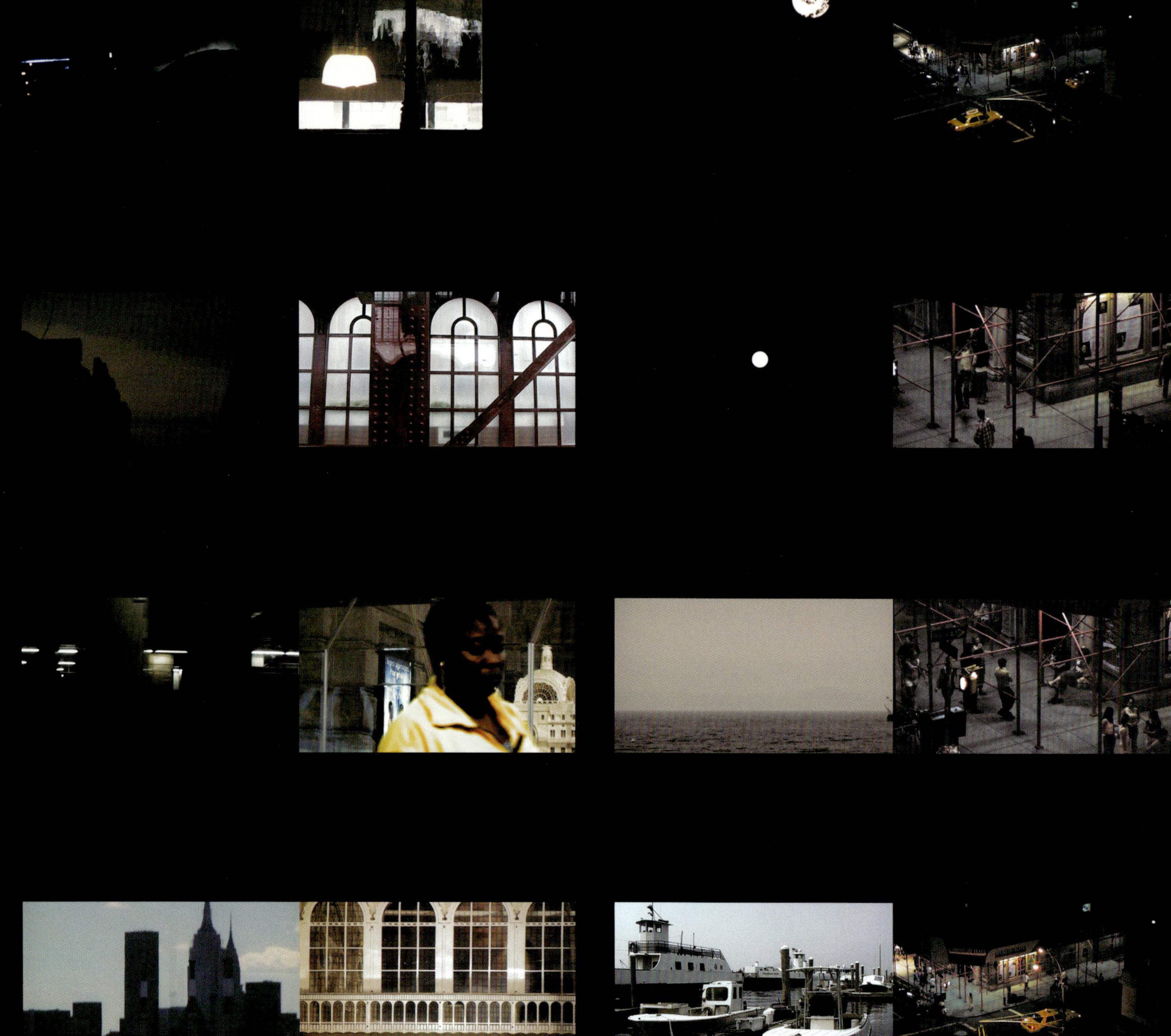

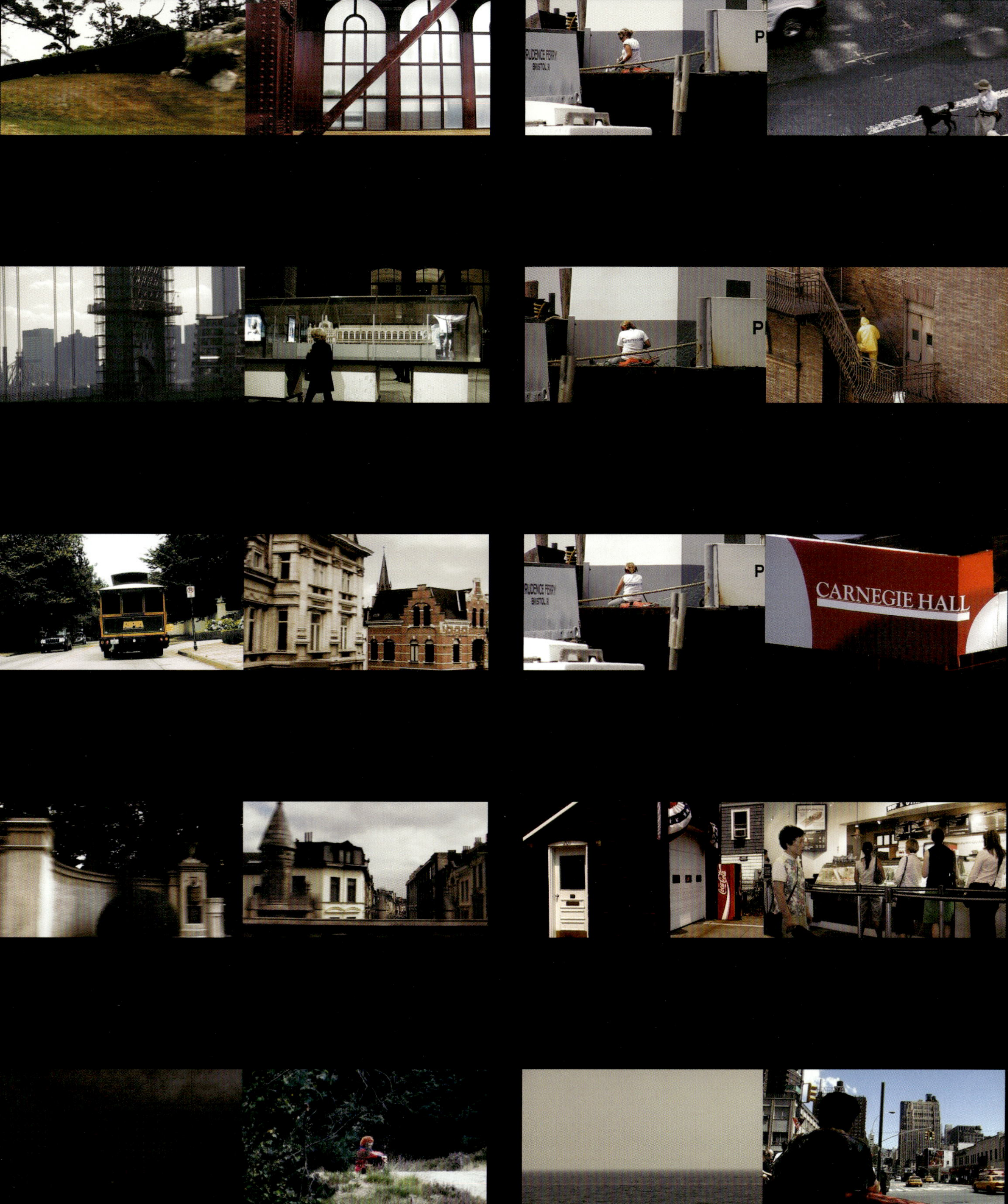
CARNEGIE HALL

J.S. Bach

No. 3 in G major, Adagio (Kandenz)

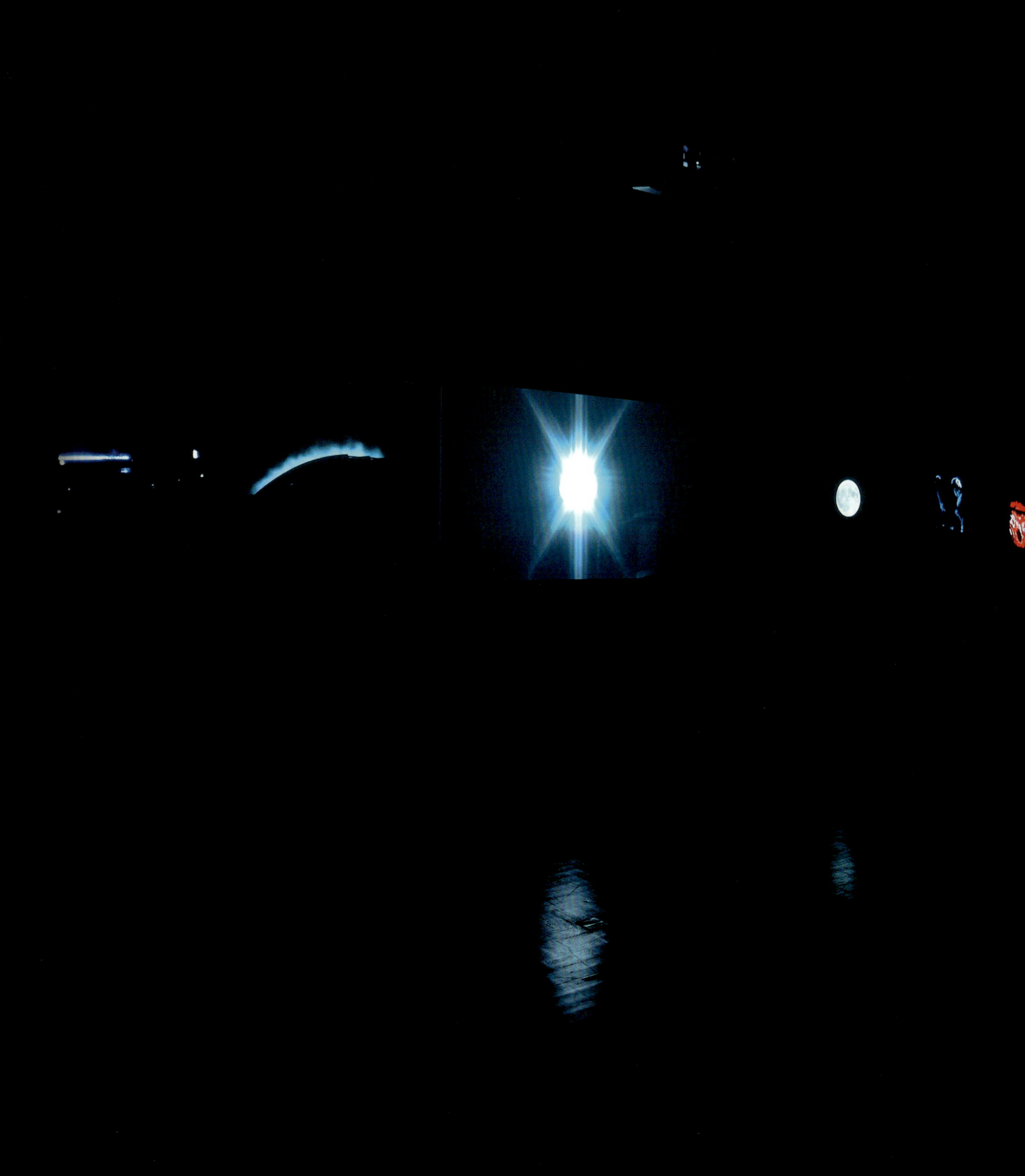

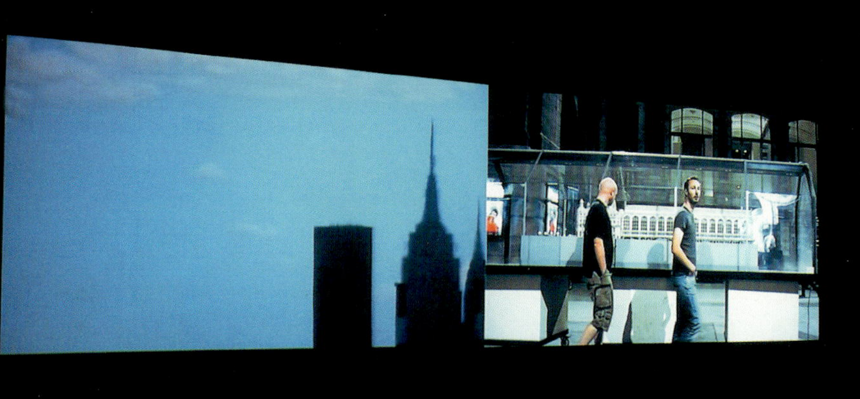
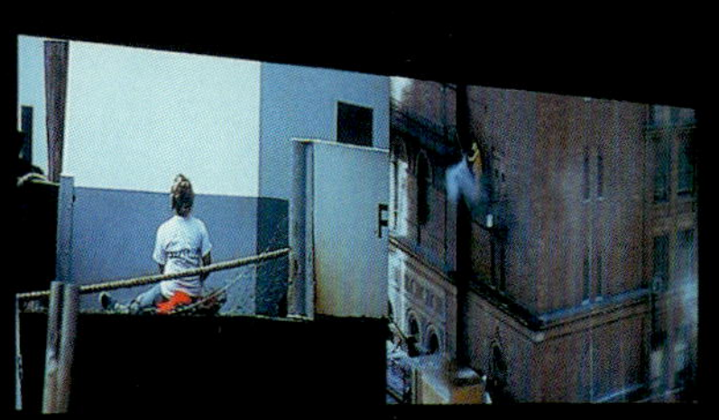

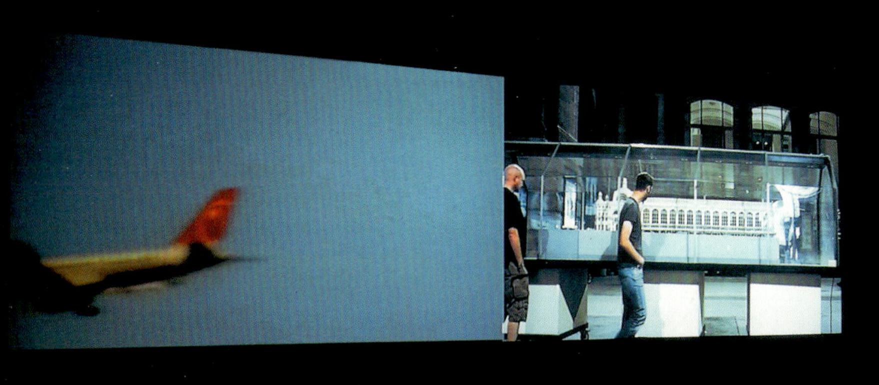
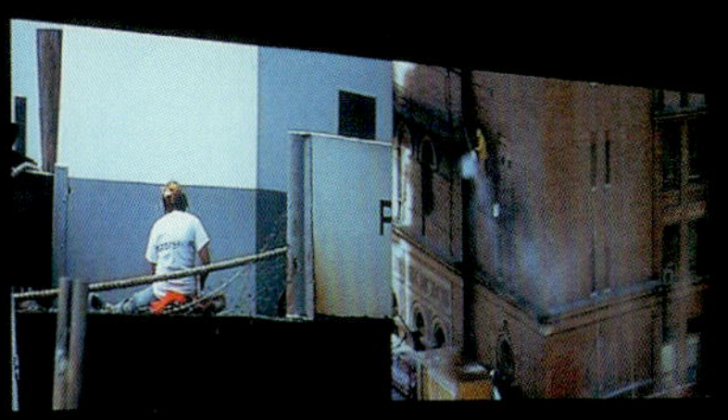
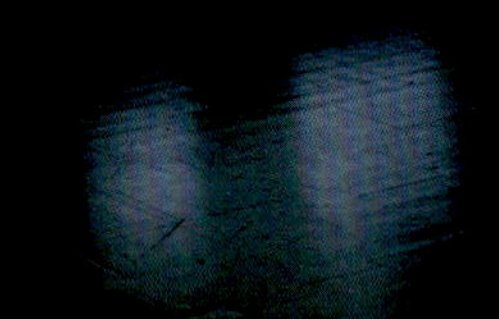

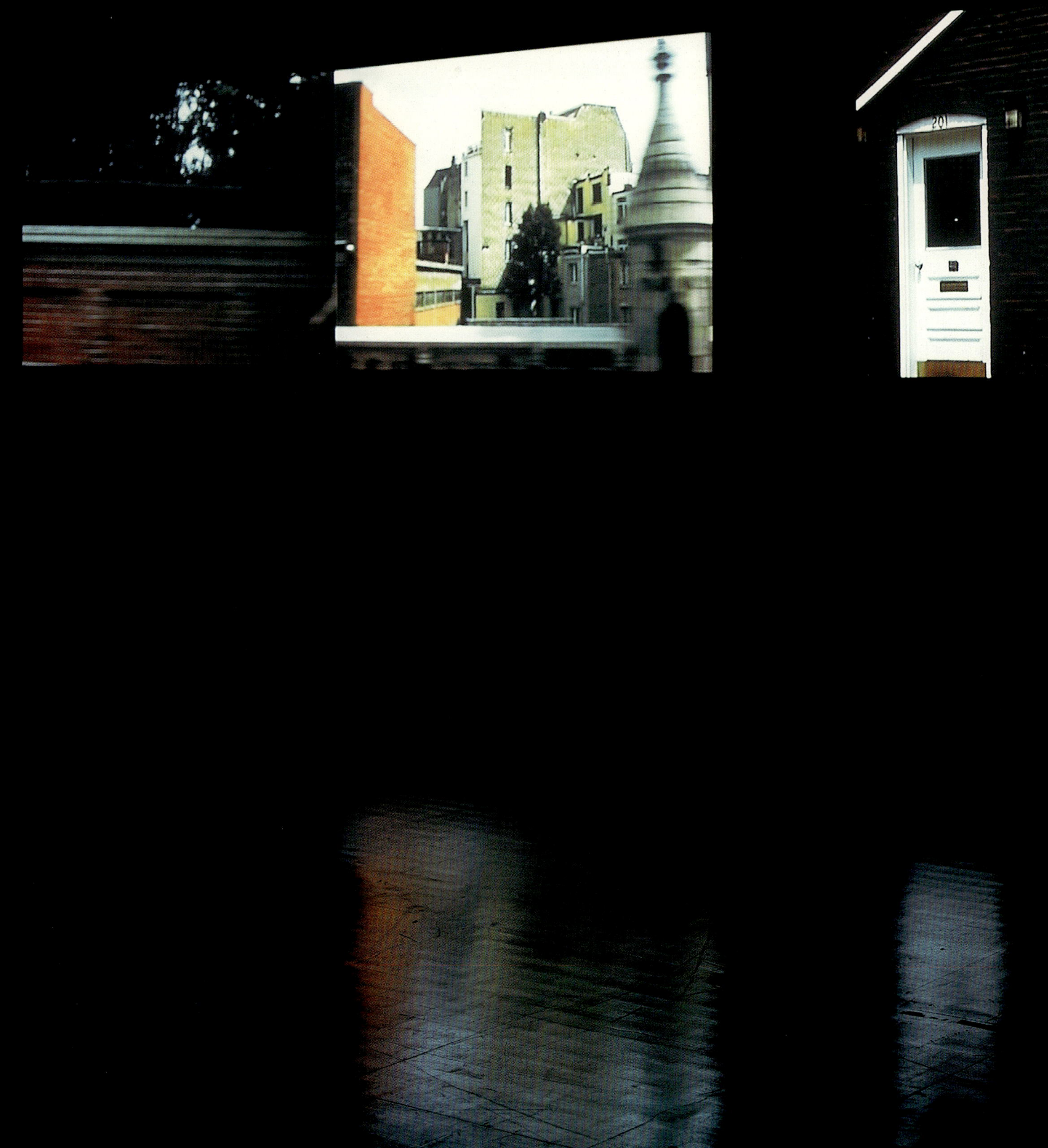
201

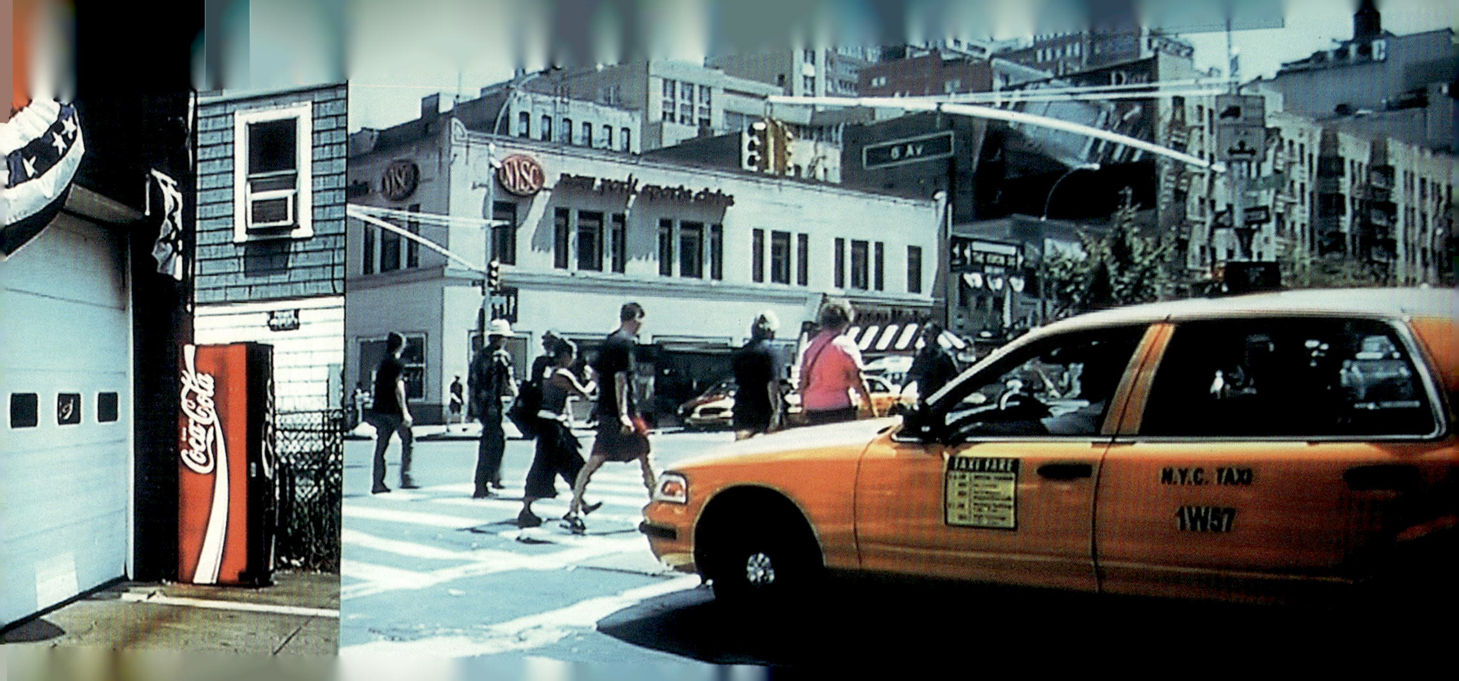
6 Av
NYSC
NYSC
new york sports clubs
Coca-Cola
Coca-Cola
TAXI FARE
N.Y.C. TAXI
1W57

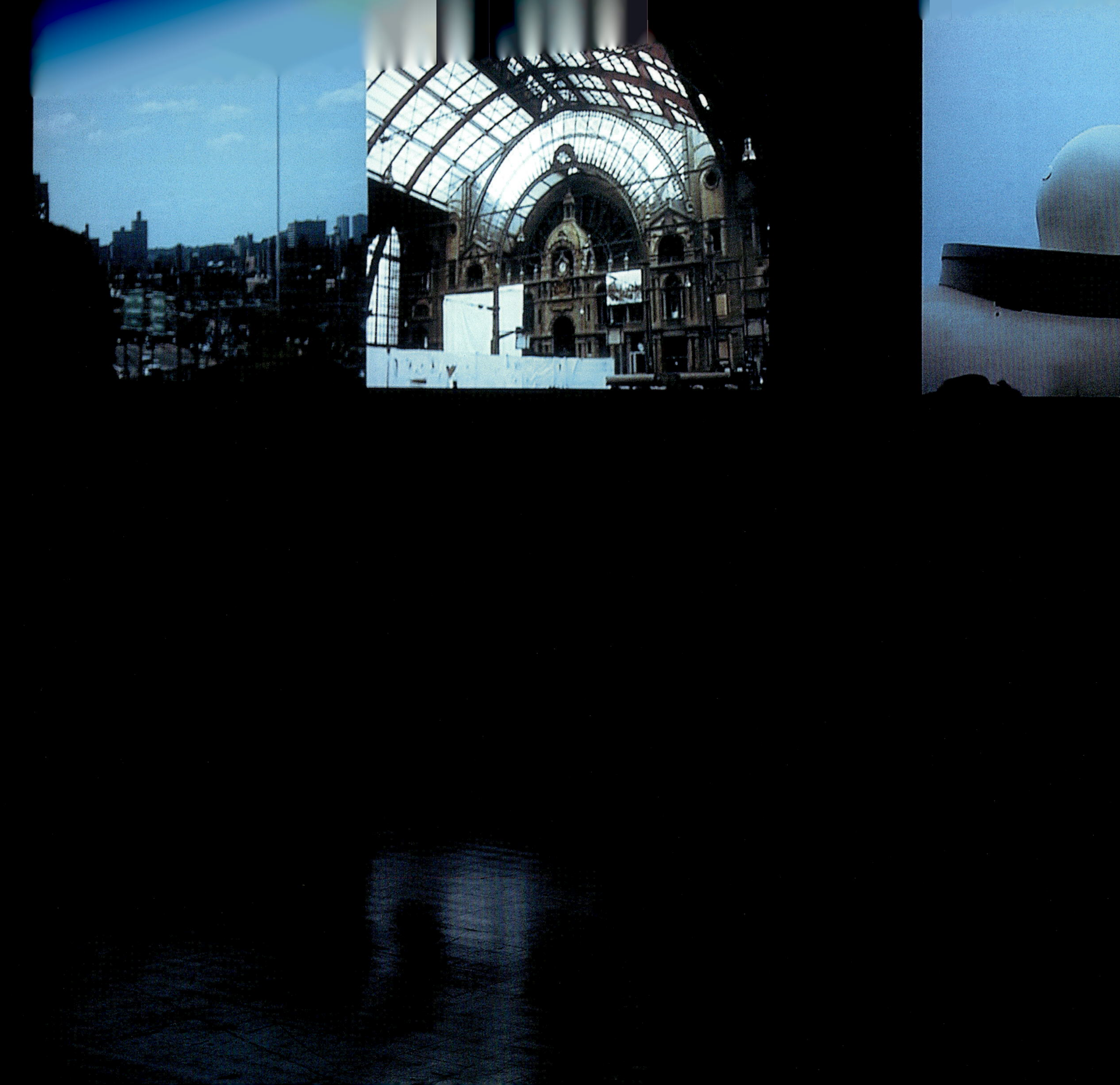

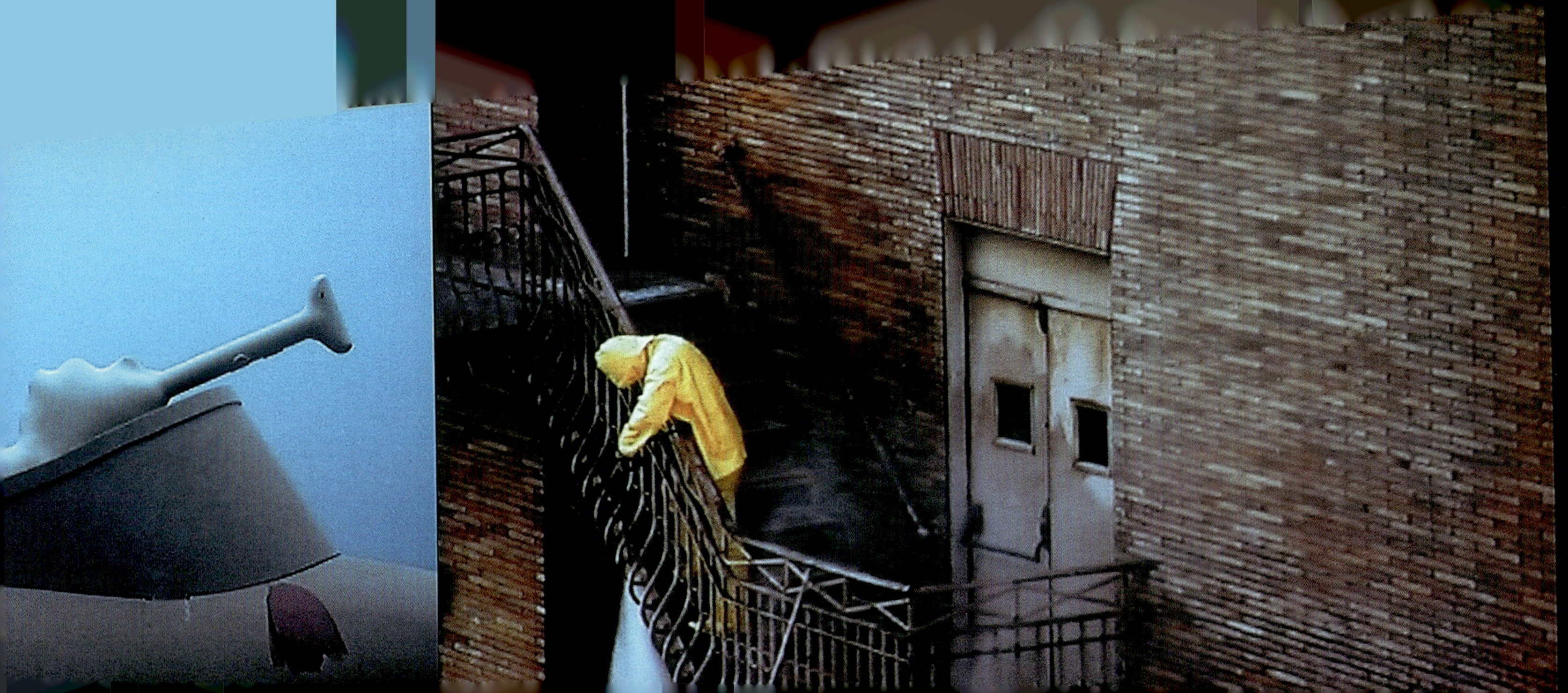

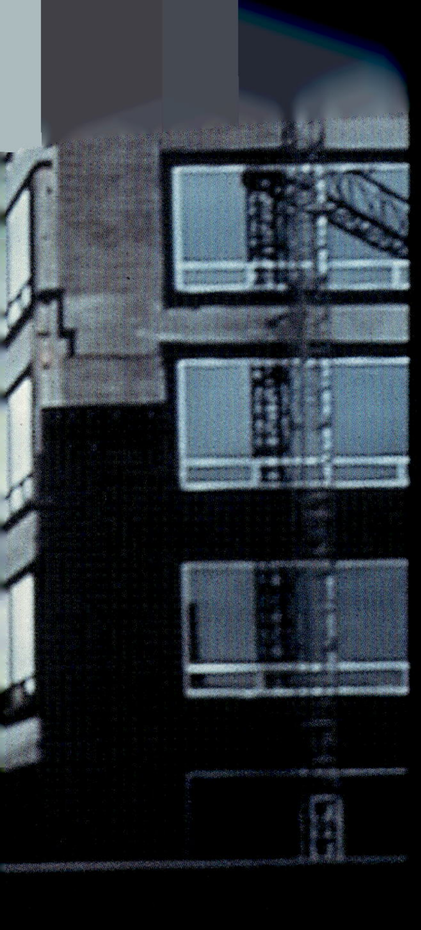

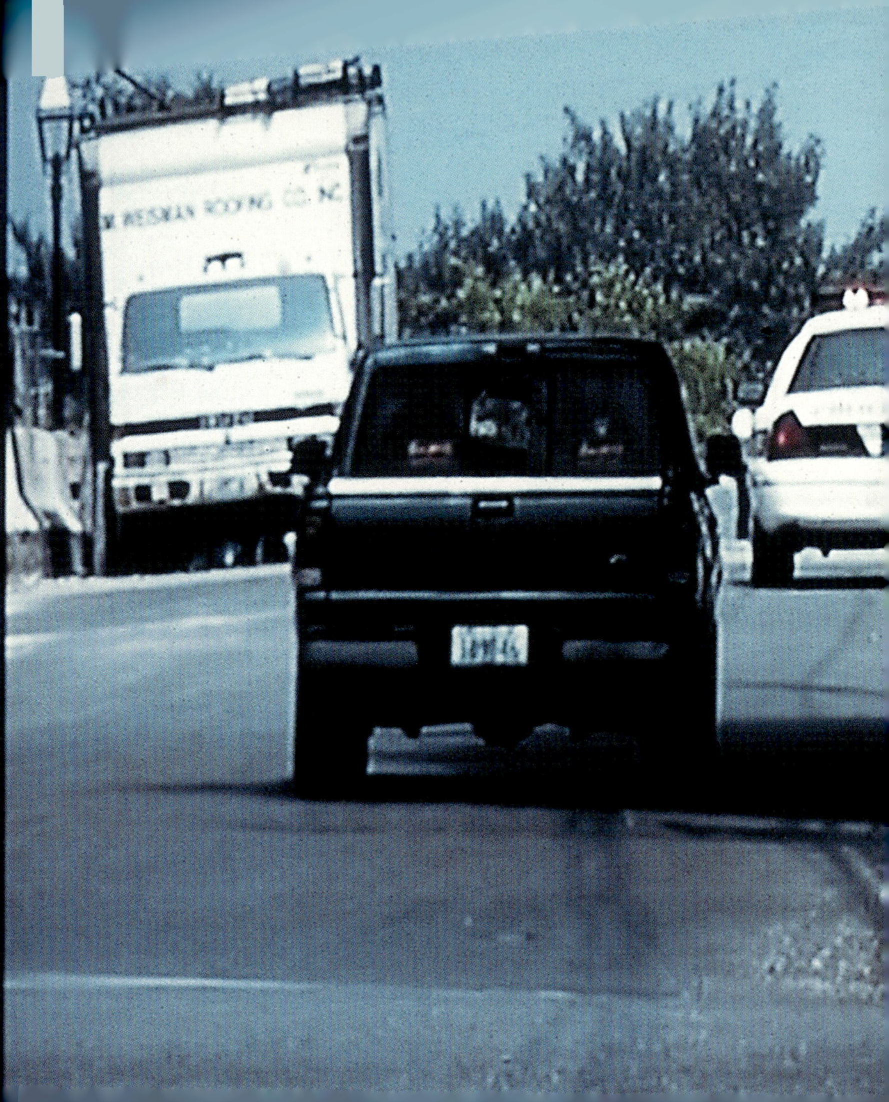

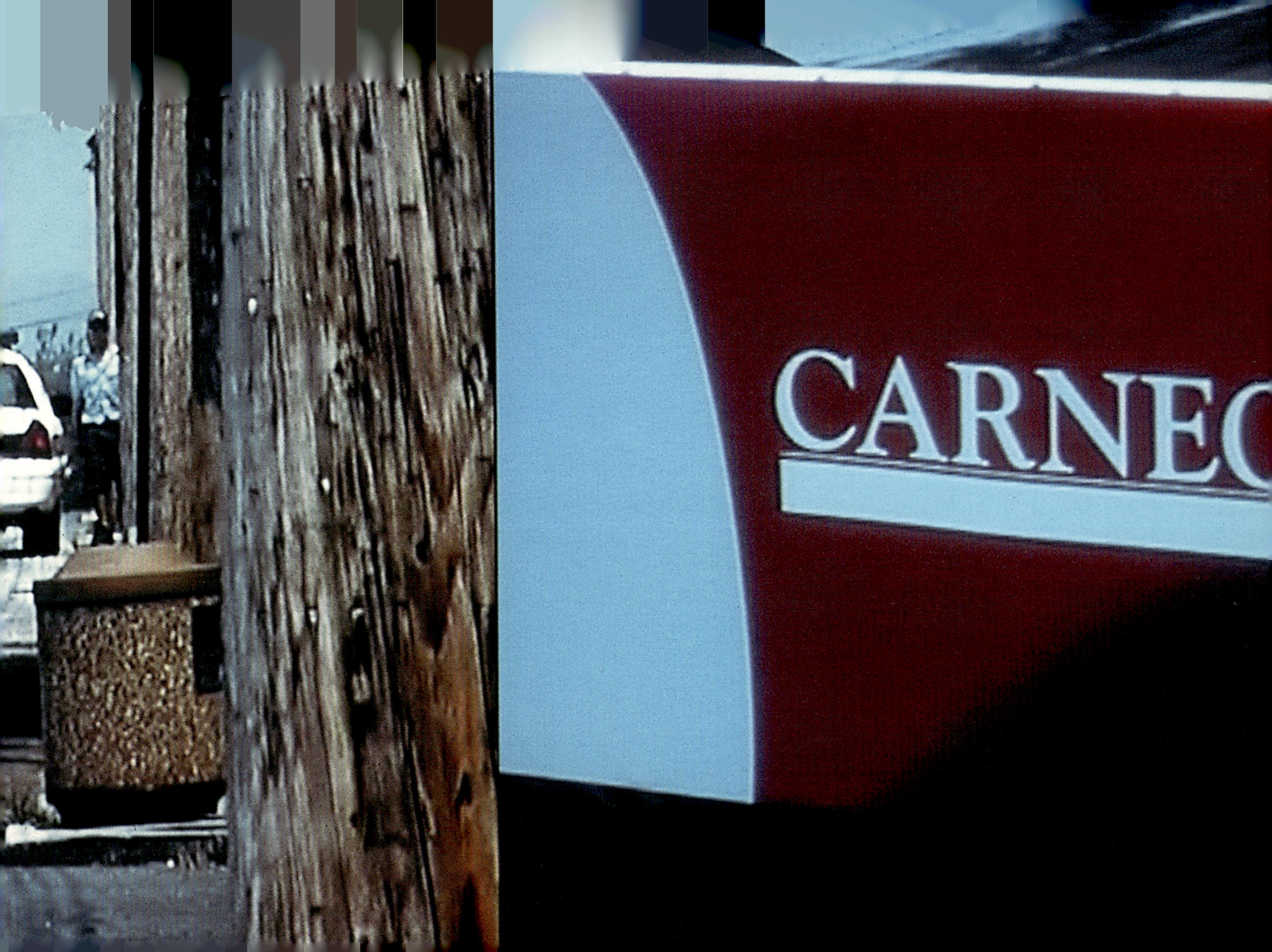
CARNE

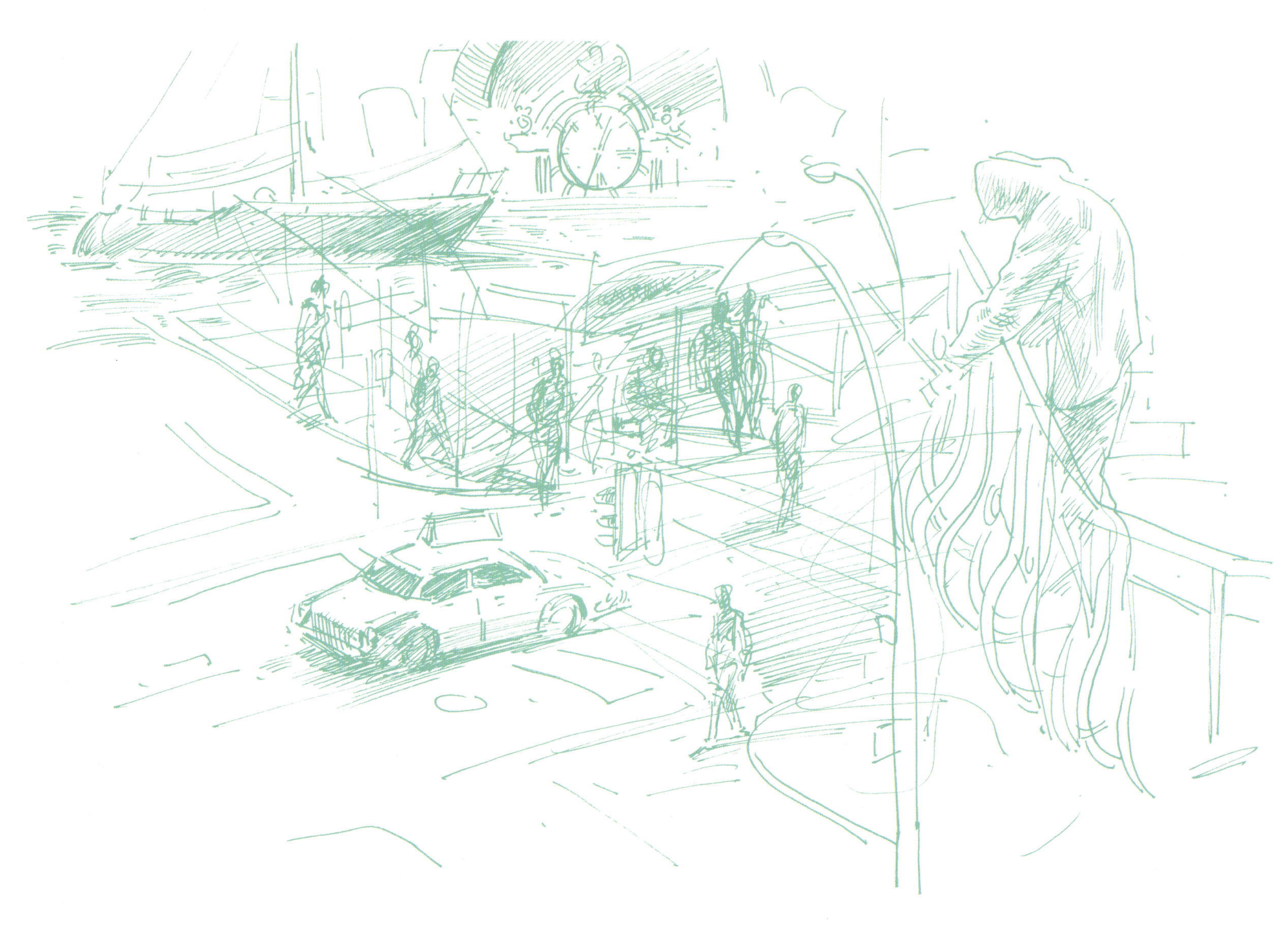

antwerp–manhattan

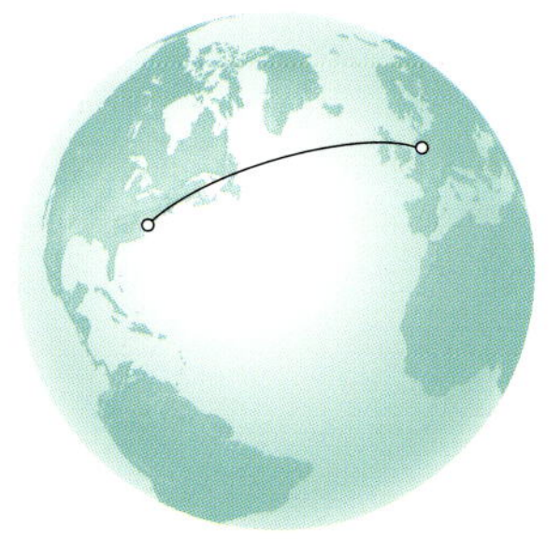

Itinerary

ℹ Antwerp Centraal Station (51° 15′N, 4° 17′E)–Carnegie Hall (40° 47′N, 73° 58′W)–Antwerp suburbs–Manhattan fringes–Rhode Island

Orientation and Sights

Centraal Station

Much more than simply a place to travel through, or a terminus, Antwerp's Centraal Station designed, in the main, by Louis Delacenserie, and built between 1895 and 1905, was commissioned by King Leopold II, and is one of the city's most imposing buildings. It is the scene for the opening of W.G. Sebald's novel *Austerlitz* in which he describes it as a 'cathedral consecrated to international trade and traffic'. Its grey and white 'medieval' turrets enhance this feeling of monumentality. The architectural jewels, though, are its vault and dome, inspired by the Pantheon in Rome, but conceived out of envy for Lucerne's new train station. Restoration of the dome, wrought from iron and glass, was begun in 1995, giving more than adequate protection to the diamond and gold shops incorporated into the station's exterior. The vault is 185m long and 44m at its highest point. Of particular interest are the luxuriant main hall with its carved escutcheons depicting corn, crossed hammers and winged wheels symbolising trade and endeavour, and the *Salon des Pas Perdu* with its gold and silver mirrors. A scale model inside the station enables one to better appreciate the magnificence of the building in its entirety.

Standing in front of the *fin de siècle* Centraal Station the elaborate neo-baroque facade seems like a literal crystallisation, in architecture, of the diamond wealth that flooded into Belgium from its African colonies around this time. Leaving the station, trains slip past more recent displays of wealth (Antwerp is a city undergoing a facelift), but also past turn-of-the-century, Old World, brownstone town houses that, in a continental drift, have translated into a New York style, on the threshold of its own modernity.

Carnegie Hall

Ten blocks from New York City's gem trading zone, the Diamond District on 47th Street, is the world famous **Carnegie Hall** at 57th and 7th. It is still the venue for the classical music loving Newport and Hamptons glitterati but now also for the newer, more street-wise bling dynasty. Over the years its renowned acoustics (for a while blunted by a hidden concrete slab inserted beneath a stage during renovation in 1986 but since removed), have enhanced the performances of musicians and singers ranging from Gustav Mahler and Judy Garland to Bob Dylan and the Beatles.

Carnegie Hall was commissioned by Andrew Carnegie and built in 1890 by architect William Burnet Tuthill. Constructed in small Roman brick with brownstone and terracotta articulations, it is one of the last edifices in Manhattan built without a steel frame, ironic given that Andrew Carnegie made his fortune out of that very commodity. The foyer spurns the baroque of certain grand buildings in favour of a restrained Brunelleschi-inspired classicism in grey and white stone. The main hall is also relatively austere and though its white is adorned with gold it is renowned more for its acoustics than its decorative style.

One can only look on enviously, a bit on the outside, and with some curiosity at this splendid cathedral built out of wealth mined from the earth. The image conjured up of this era of pioneering drifts as one leaves town: on arrival in Rhode Island one mansion follows another on Ocean Drive, a lonesome yacht sails by, out of the picture, destination uncertain…

Simon Harvey

Helios	Khufu	Artemis	Zeus
Pharos	Nebo	Maussollos	Icarus
Ulysses	Jason	Quartermaine	Kurtz
A. Cravan	B. Traven	Bas Jan A	Crowhurst D

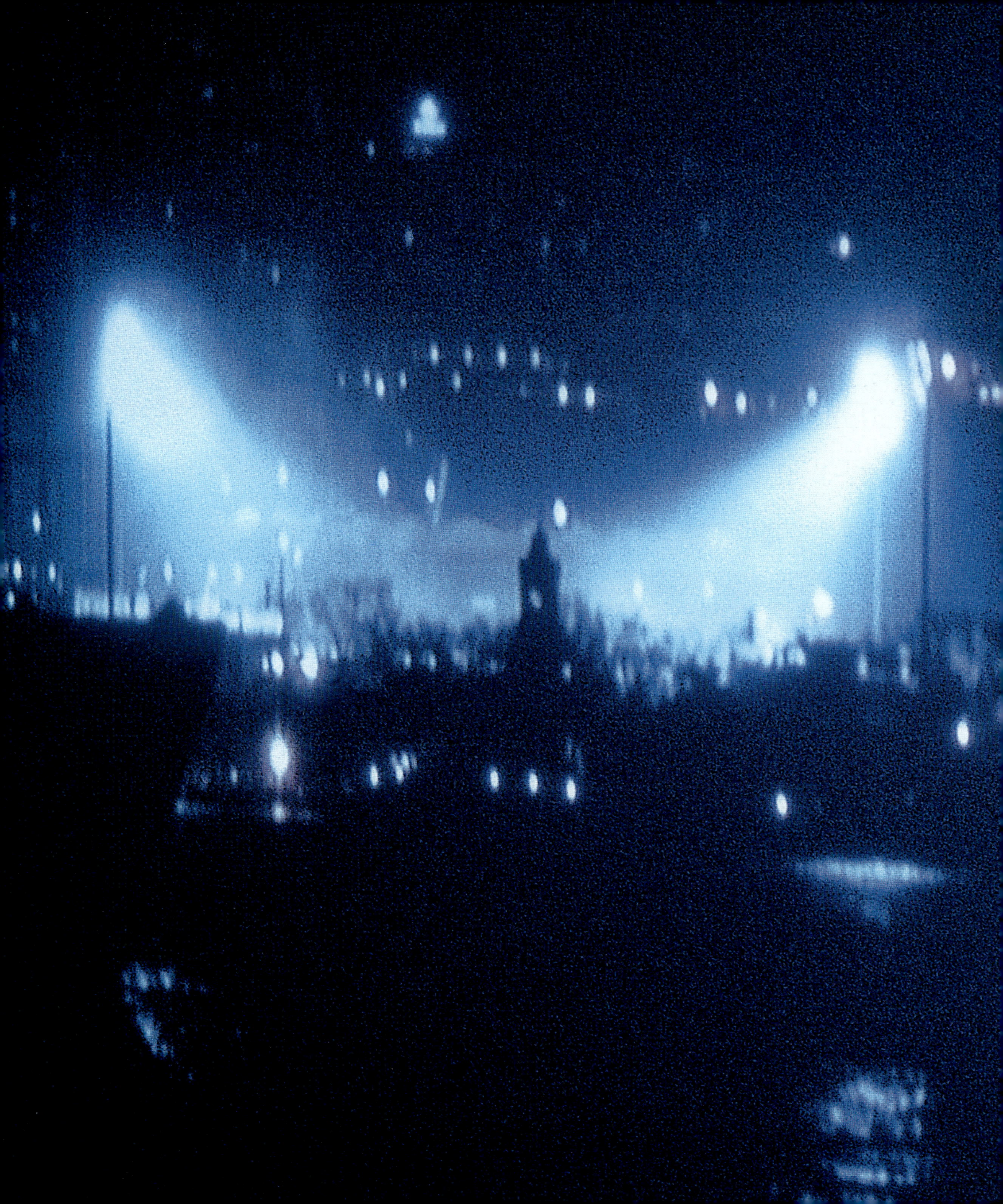

Downward Straits

Downward Straits (2004)
Four-screen video installation, four channels sound
Running time: 13:25min, continuous loop
Dimensions variable: rear projection screens
Installation view: Leeds City Art Gallery, 2005

— Sector Türkeli, sector Türkeli. *Kunamar, Kunamar.*
— *Kunamar,* sector Türkeli.

— We are twenty miles to the pilot station. Our ETA is 1300. Over.
— Standby *Kunamar,* standby.
— South of the Princess Islands, south of the Princess Islands.
— *Kunamar, Kunamar,* sector Türkeli.

— Sector Türkeli, this is *Kunamar* come in.
— What is your call sign, call sign please?
— Time Three, Echo, Alpha, Good, Nine. Over.

— *Kunamar,* understood. What is your length overall?
— Length overall 180 meters. Over.
— What is your maximum manoeuvring speed in Istanbul strait?
— Istanbul strait, manoeuvring speed can go up to eleven Knots. Over.
— Do you have dangerous cargo on board?
— No dangerous cargo on board.
— Do you require pilot for Istanbul strait?
— Yes, pilot for Istanbul strait. Over.
— *Kunamar,* what is your last port and your next port?
— Last port Ilyichevsk, Ukraine. Next port is Bussan, Korea. Over.
— *Kunamar,* understood. What is your ETA, a beam of Türkeli lighthouse?
— ETA of beam Türkeli lighthouse 1300. Over.
— Understood *Kunamar,* please proceed to ten miles, and stay adrift. We will inform you.
— Understood, we will proceed up to ten miles of the Türkeli lighthouse,
and then I am waiting for your information. Thank you.
— Thank you, *Kunamar.*
— *Argo, Argo,* motor vessel *Argo,* this is sector Kadıköy. Over.
— This is *Argo.*

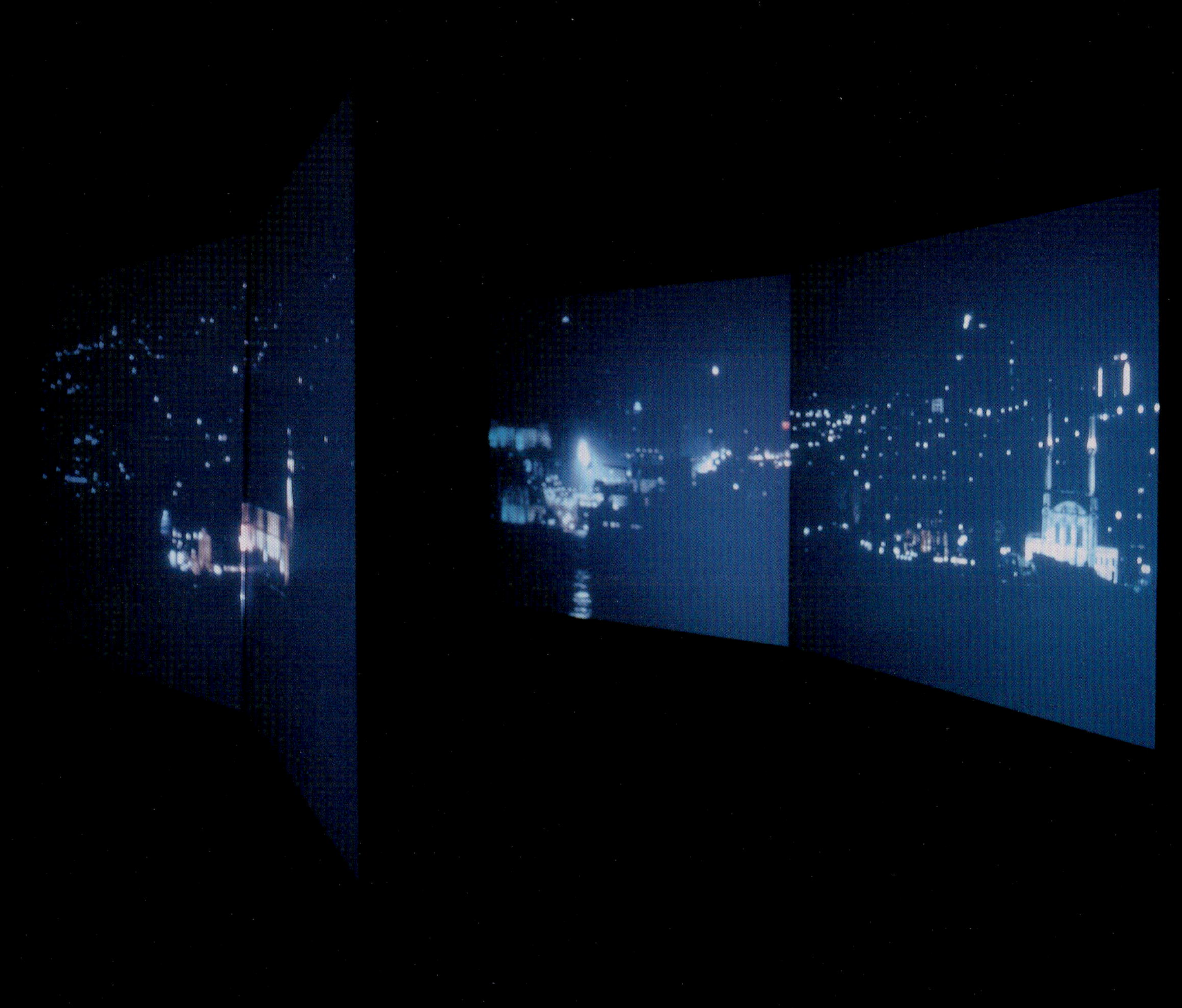

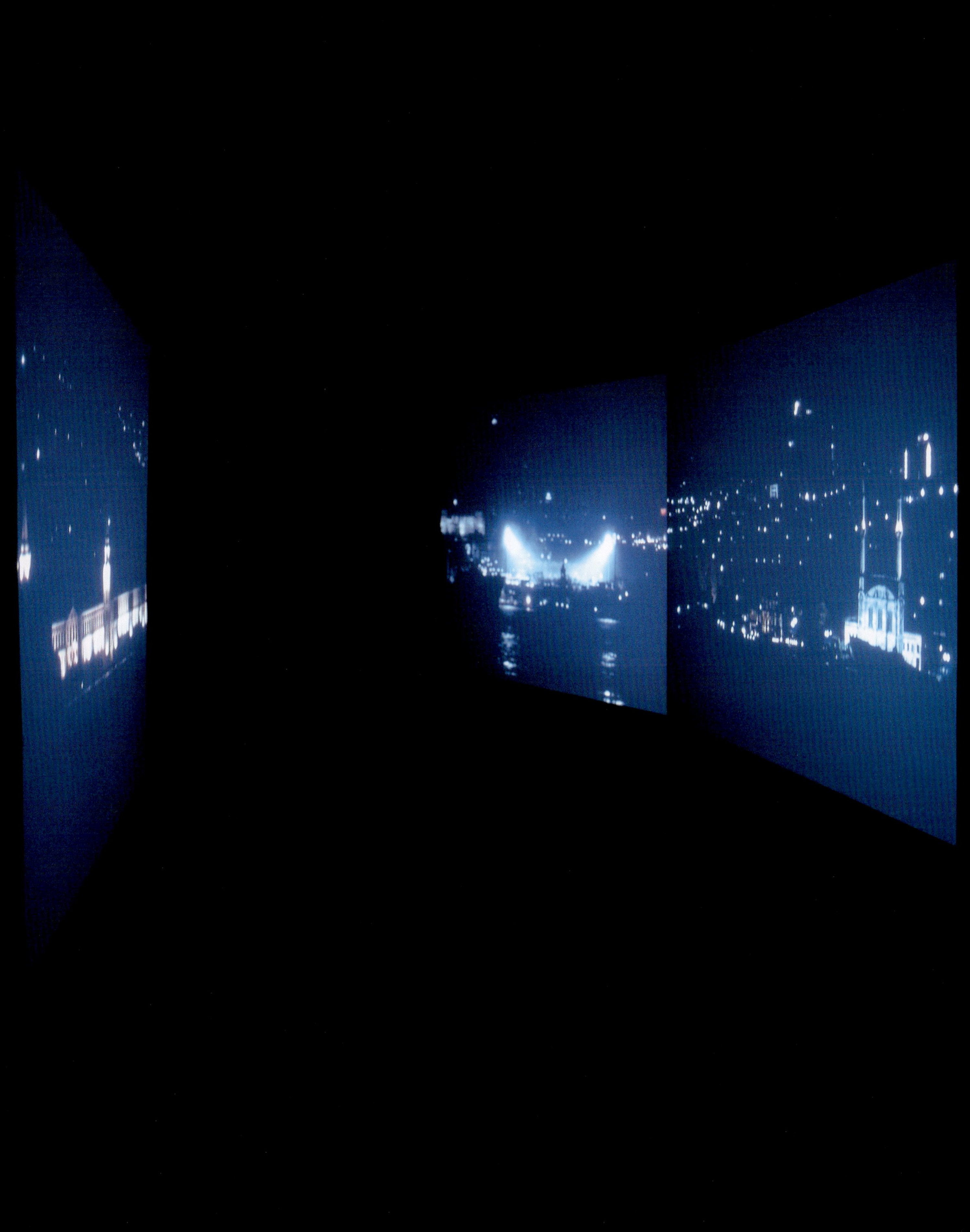

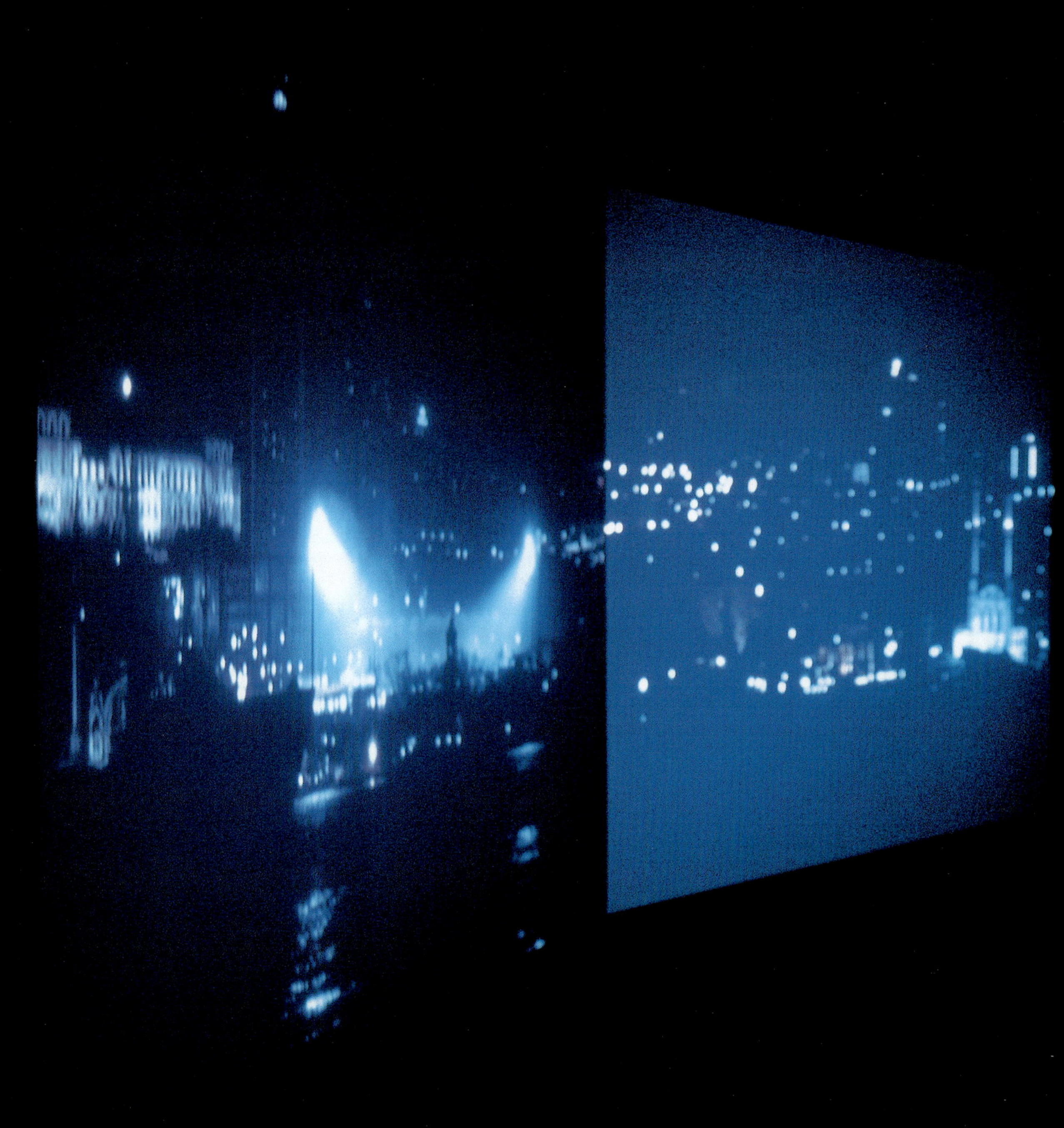

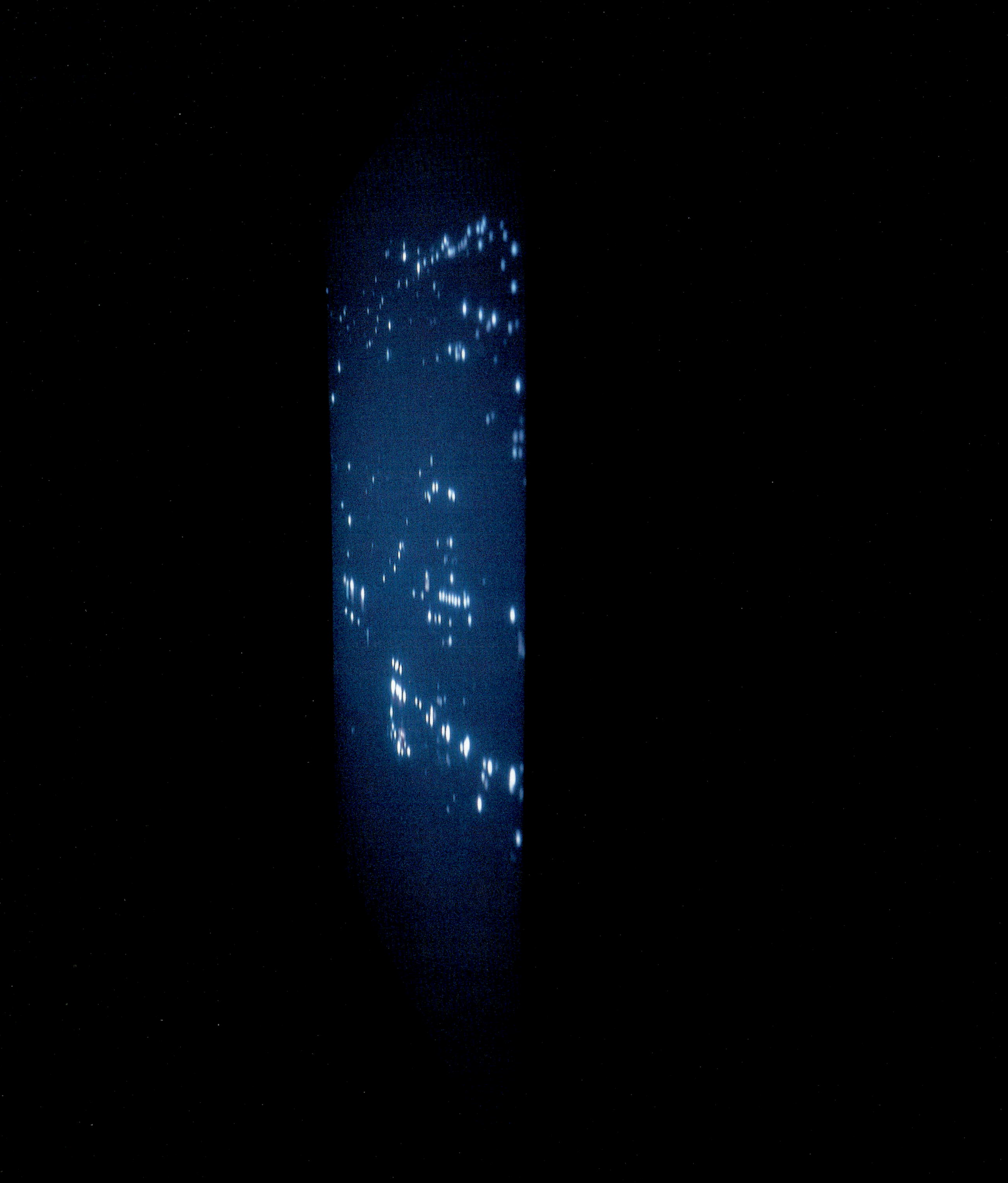

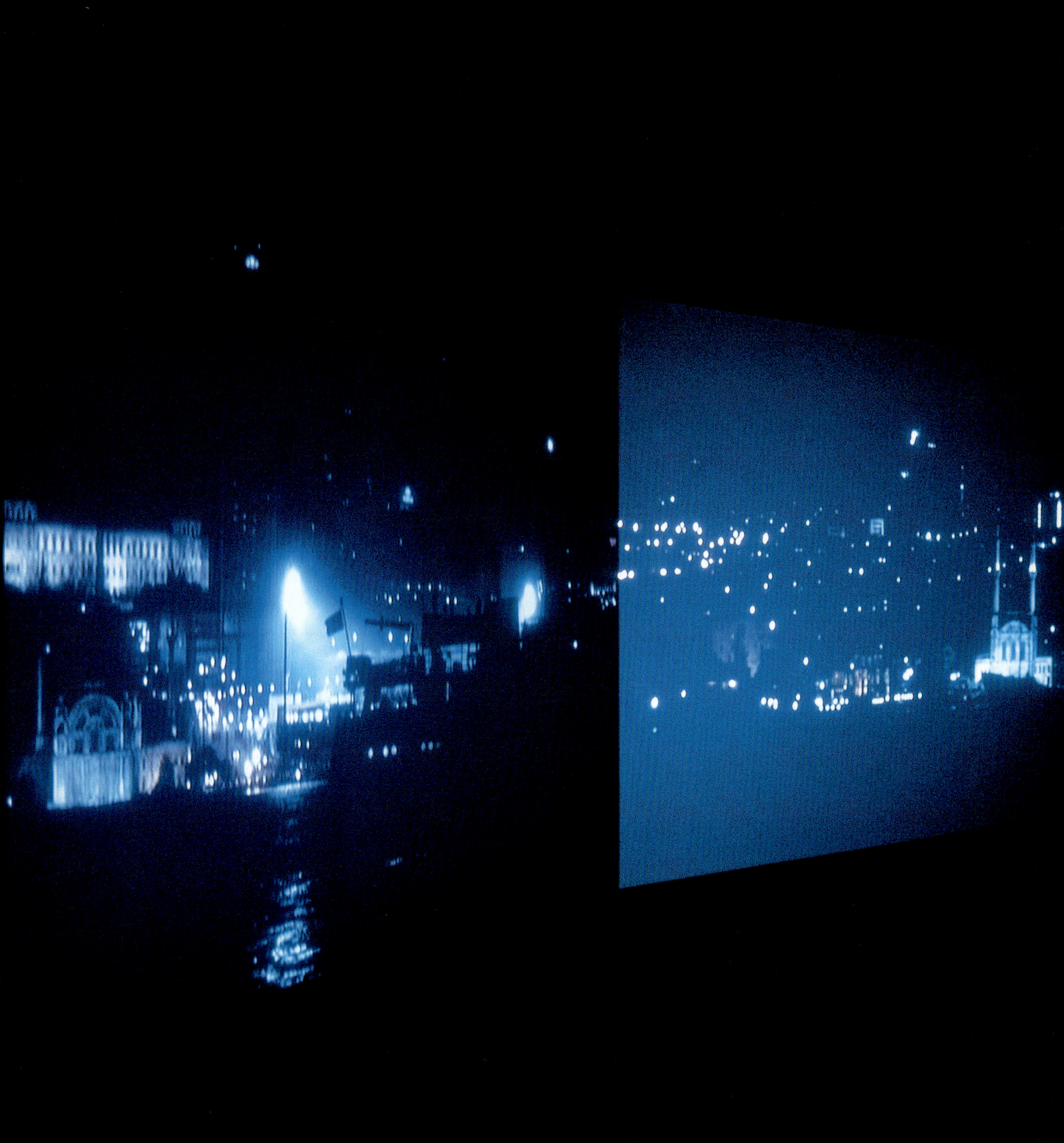

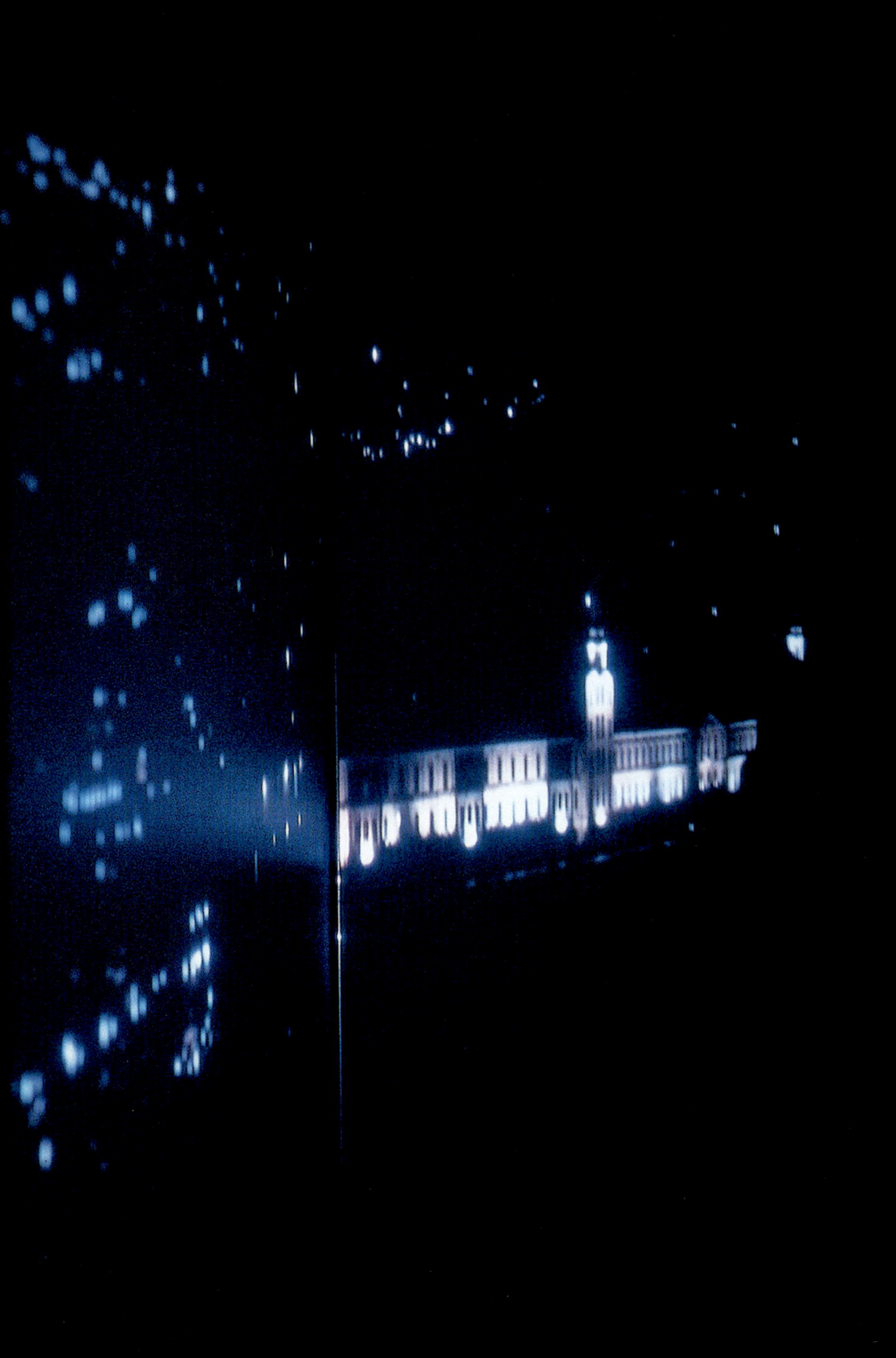

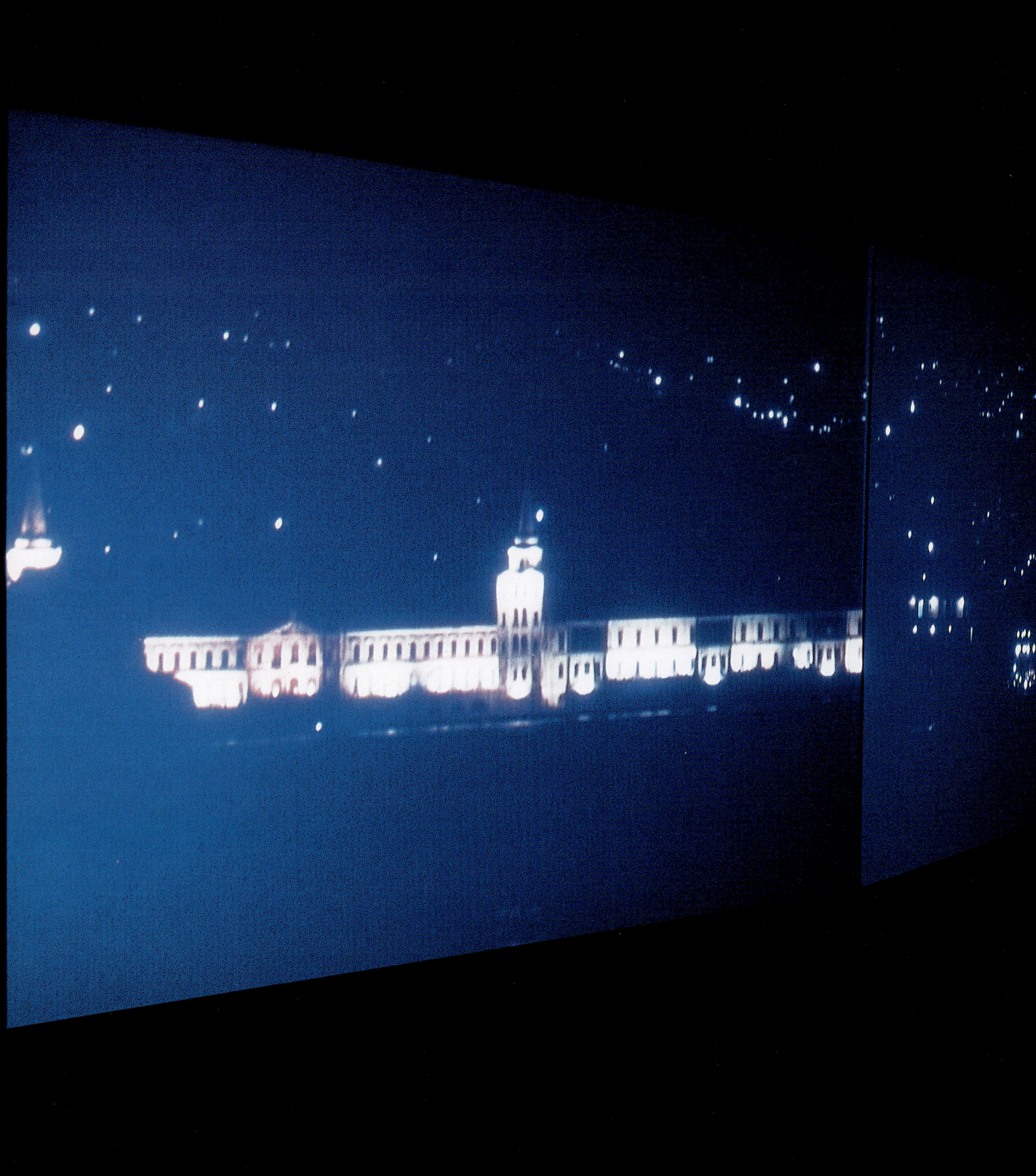

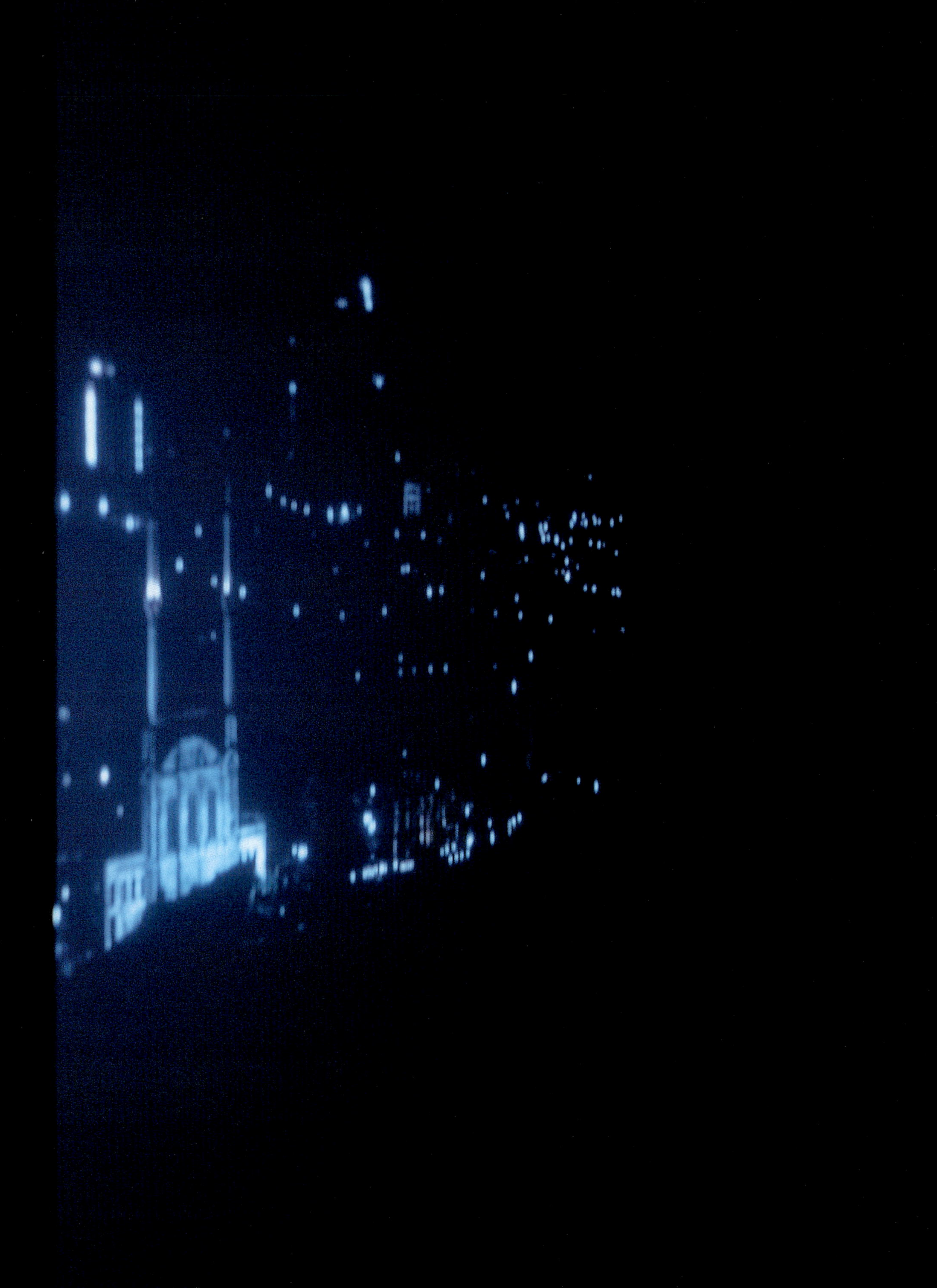

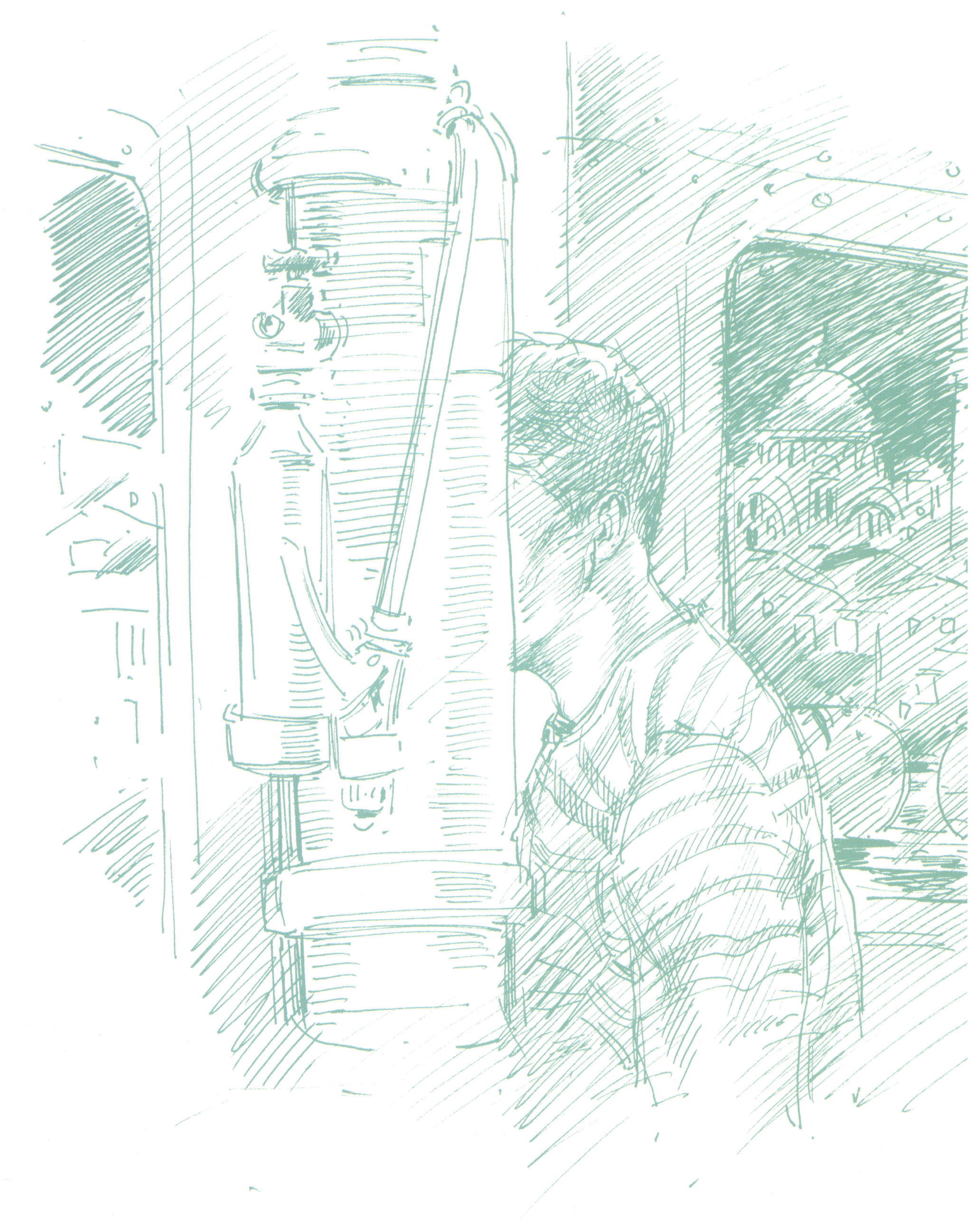

the bosphorus

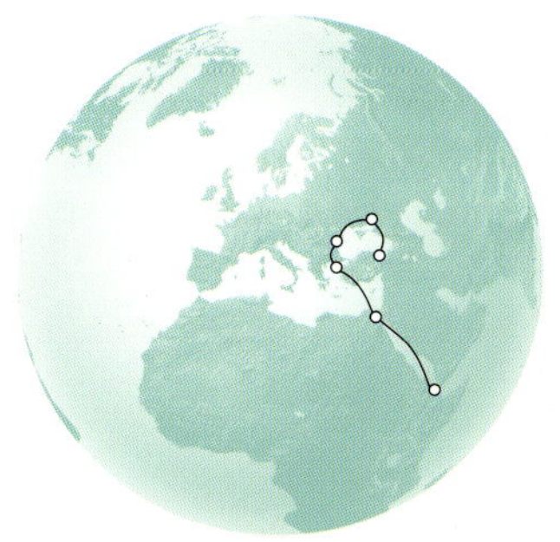

Itinerary

ℹ Points South–Bab al-Mandab (10° 28′N, 40° 37′E)–Suez (30° 0′N, 32° 35′E)–Mediterranean (Crusader, Delta, Matruh, Jason, Aegean)–Dardanelles (40° 0′N, 26° 15′E)–Sea of Marmara–Bosphorus (28° 50′E, 40° 58′N)–Black Sea (Danube, Georgia)–Varna–Odessa–Kerch Strait–Sea of Azov (45° 6′N, 36° 35′E)–Rostov–Trabzon (40° 55′N, 39° 50′E)

Southern Approaches

Beyond the Suez Canal, which divides Asia and Africa, ships enter the Mediterranean and, sailing up past the Dodecanese and Cyclades into the Aegean Sea, they are channelled towards the Dardanelles, or Hellespont as it was formerly known. The sea, which flows in both directions through the straits (on the surface towards the Aegean and as an undercurrent towards the Marmara) seems to portend the shifting currents of history. First one comes to the ancient archaeological site of Troy, on the Asiatic side, and then the First World War battlefield site at Gallipoli, almost Europe. Steaming north, leaving behind the wreckage of love and war, you enter the Sea of Marmara, dotted with the so-called 'marble islands', and the approaches to the fabled city of Constantinople, now Istanbul.

Orientation and Sights

Istanbul offers up some unusual vistas, not least at night from the strange channel of the Bosphorus where several sites shine out like beacons. Besides the Blue Mosque, Hagia Sofia and the Topkapı Palace, there are spectacular lesser-known sights. Some are closer to the water such as the Ottoman baroque style Ortaköy Mosque and that grand neo-classical academy the Kuleli Barracks, while others command views over the straits like the University of the Bosphorus on the hill in the Bebek district. The resounding noise of the BJK Inönü Stadium, home to FC Beşiktaş, is articulated by the waterfront grandeur of the Dolmabahçe Palace in front of it. Out of the glare are mysterious hidden bazaars such as Tahtakale, the informal currency market where the real business of Turkey is done, but where tourists might still find a bargain.

The Bosphorus, or 'Ox Passage', the world's narrowest strait, is a monumental waterway in more ways than one. It is 30km long and crossed by two bridges, the Bogaziçi (1074m long) and the Fatih Sultan Mehmet (1090m) 5km to the north, otherwise known as Bosphorus bridges I and II, and also by a subterranean rail link, passing through the Marmaray tunnel. Xerxes crossed the water in 480 BC to invade the West; Alexander in 334 BC to conquer lands to the East. It is famously known as the line dividing Europe (*Rumeli*) and Asia (*Anadolu*). In reality, as a border, it is as much glided along as passed across. Monumental Stamboul, going about its own business, turns a blind eye to more or less legal transits to and from Varna, Odessa, Rostov and Turkey's own Black Sea ports such as Trabzon. The Bosphorus is marked in legend. It was, perhaps, the channel through which the waters poured in both the myths of Gilgamesh and the Bible. Today the flood of cheap goods in both directions is punctuated only by errant navigation. Over 90 per cent of shipwrecks occur on the northern approaches beyond the Anatolian lighthouse, including a recent wreck in 2003, the Georgian vessel *Svyatoy Panteleymon*, but many remember the Russian tanker *Volgoneft* that split in two in 1999 leaving its mark on the Sea of Marmara.

The **Ortaköy Mosque**, commissioned in 1853 by Sultan Abdulmecid, and built by Armenian architect Nikoğos Balyan, has two minarets and a dome adorned on the inside with pink mosaics. As with many other Ottoman mosques, it has both harem and hunkar quarters (a type of royal lodge or gallery).

Over the water on the Asian side, built in 1845 and also founded by Abdulmecid, are the **Kuleli Barracks** which once housed the military academy. In 1941 the Transportation Command was housed here to control and communicate with ships traversing the isthmus.

Simon Harvey

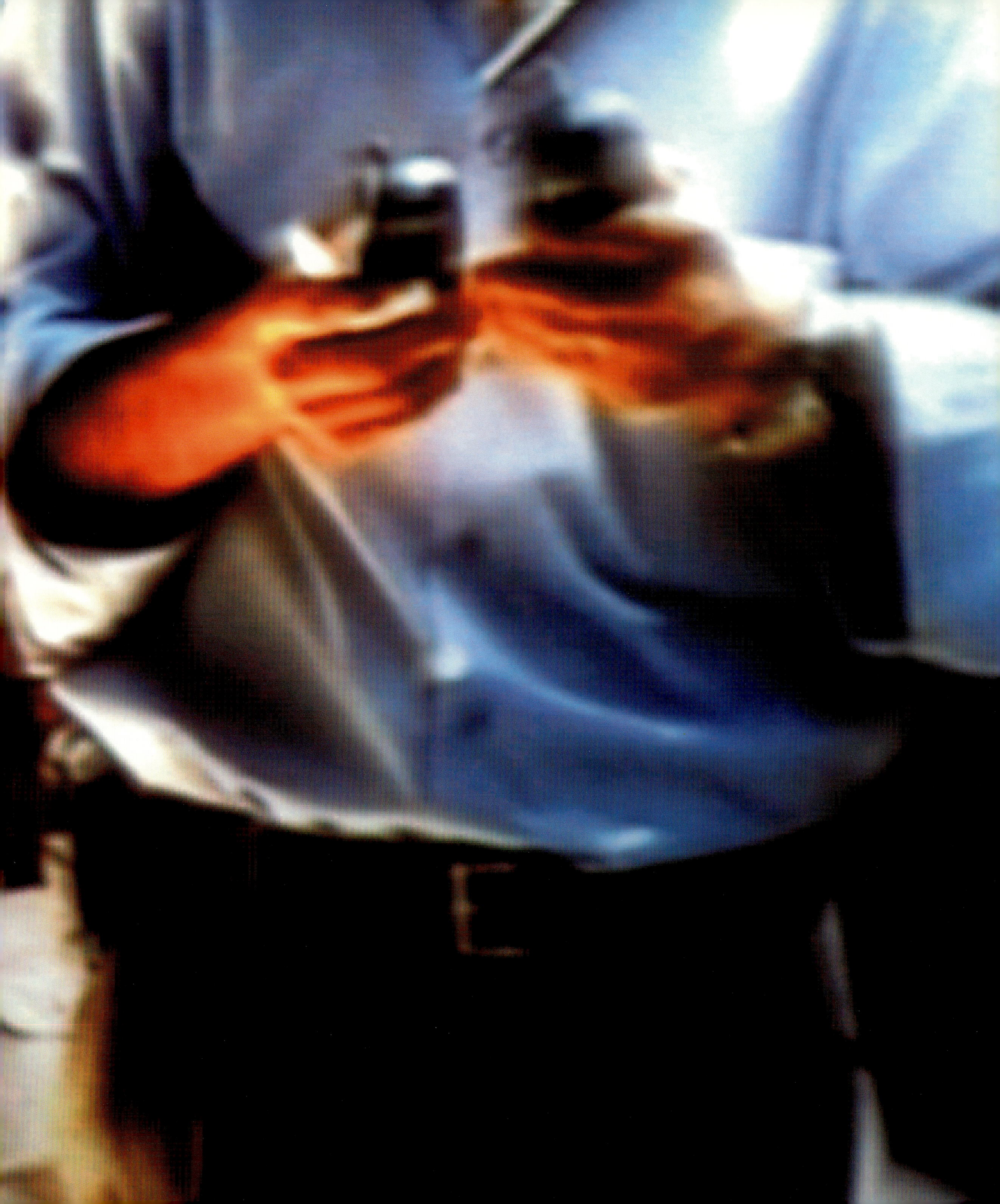

Tahtakale

Tahtakale (2004)
Four-screen video installation, four channels sound
Running time: 08:01min, continuous loop
Dimensions variable: front/rear projection screens
Installation view: Nottingham Castle, Nottingham, 2006

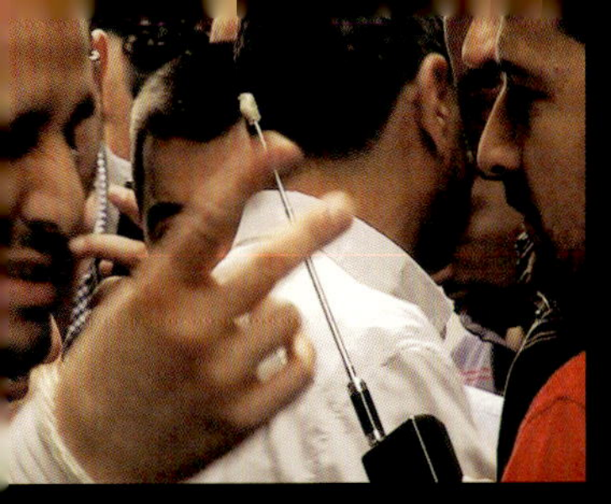

Is anybody selling exact?
I've got exact.
Abdullah Bey is leading the way.
Yes, Sir.
Shh, what happened?
Ismail what are you saying?
Buy for fifteen.
Hot, hot simiiit!
We are ready, buy for tomorrow.
I buy all sorts, all sorts, ready for 35.
Ready, ready buy for $35, ready for Thursday.
200 to 100. Hit the fucking thing.
Ridvan, how much is it?
My friend, go a bit this way.
Mr Hasan will buy all sorts.
Ready, it's 2 o'clock, 4, 5?
Have you got anything, brother?
There is some, ready for $60.

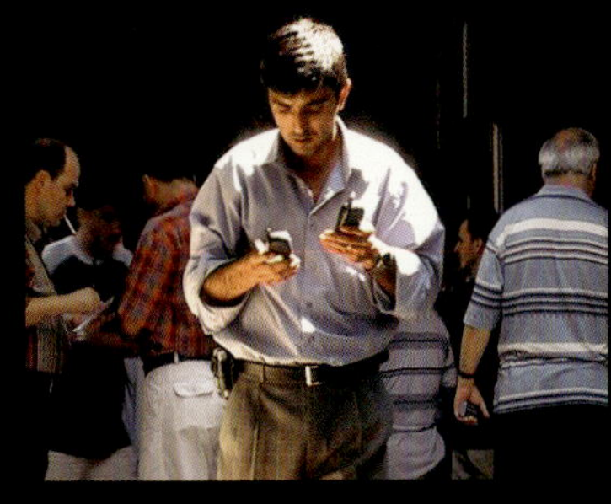

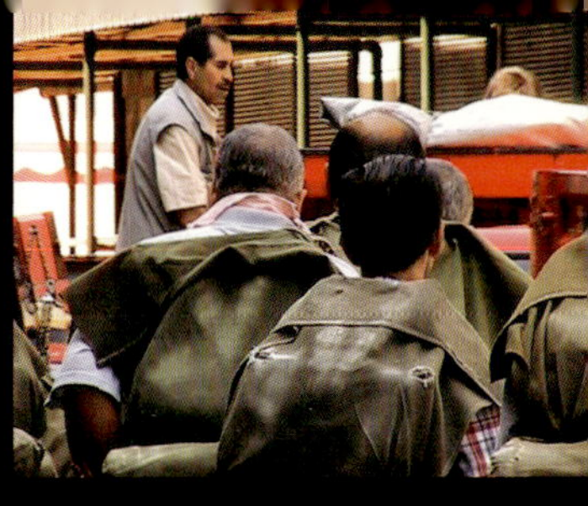

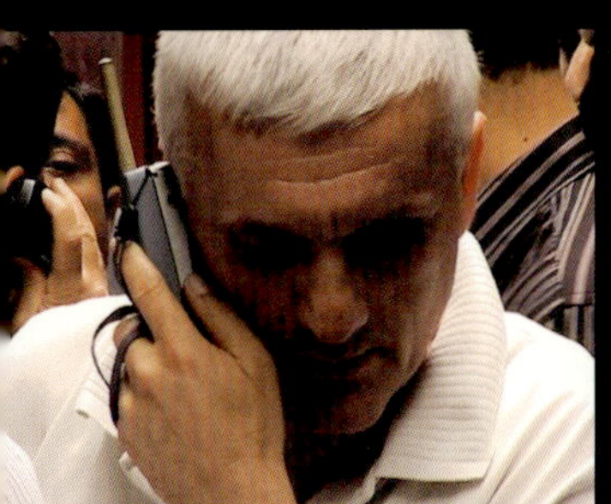

I buy all sorts.
I'll buy ready.
Buy for Monday.
Exact, I've got exact Euros.
Hot, hot simiiit!
If the interest is two million per month,
fucking multiply it, 100 000.
It's necessary that the banks load it. And if
the interest is 50%?
You wouldn't buy dollars this time.
Euros, is anybody selling Euros?
Gentlemen, I'm going. What are you saying,
it's ready?
Ahmet Bey, it's ready to buy for Friday,
for tomorrow.
I am buying Euros with cash. Euros.
With cash!
Exact, I've got exact Euros.

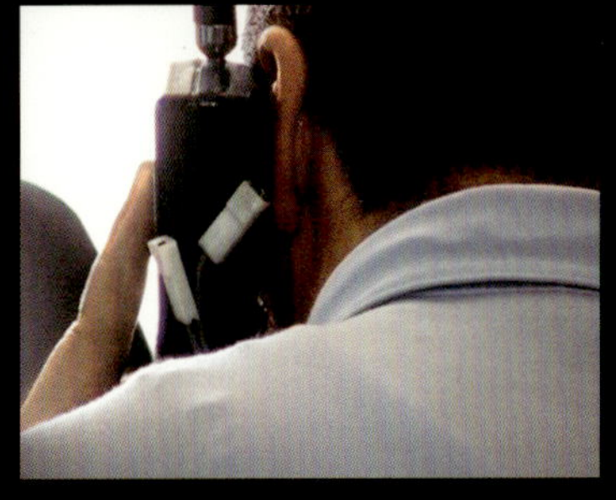

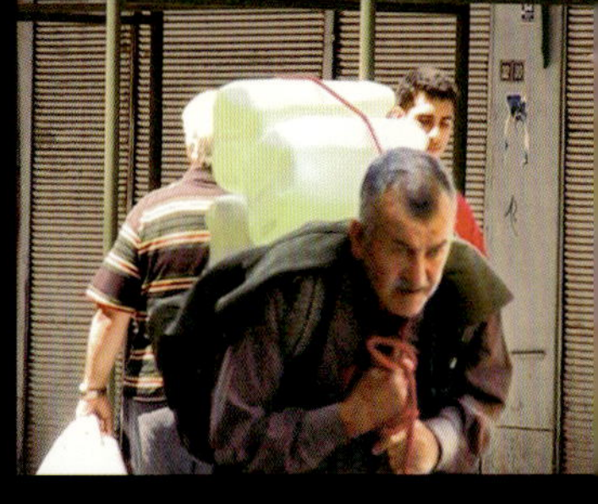

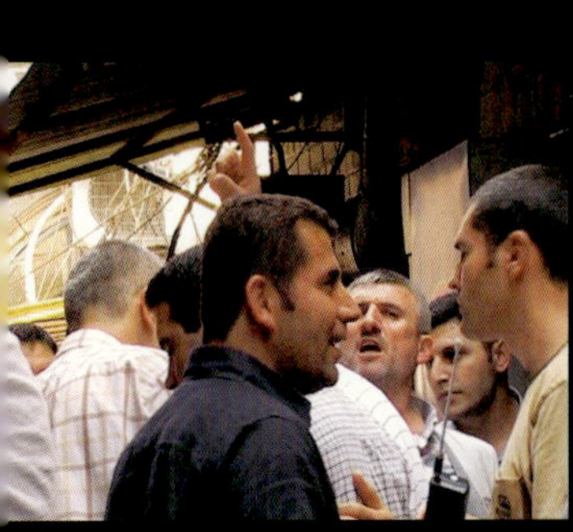

Cuneyt, Cuneyt, Cuneyt… send it ah.
Hello, are you in the shop?
10 million – 15 million – what can you get?
100 million points.
If it is two million, multiply the fucker.
Zafer!
It will be good to note this. There is definitely
going to be a crisis for fuck's sake.
Definitely a crisis…
Don't tell me that nobody is interested;
we've been going for two days.
How much is it? Two billions?
Half, half.
What's happened boy?
The banks started increasing it again,
increasing it again.
Doesn't he have a telephone?
Exact Euros, 10 000 pieces exact Euros.

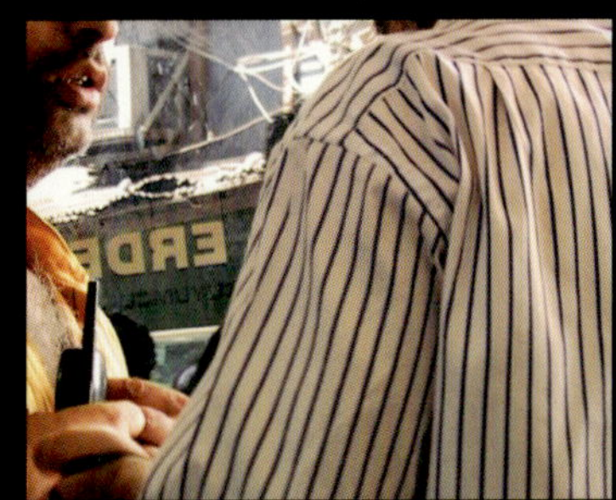

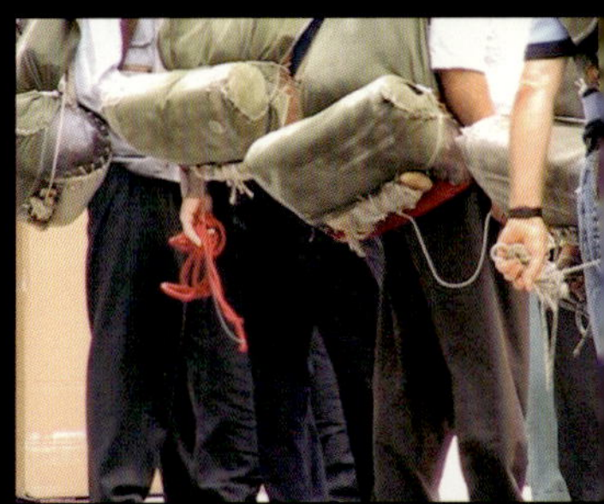

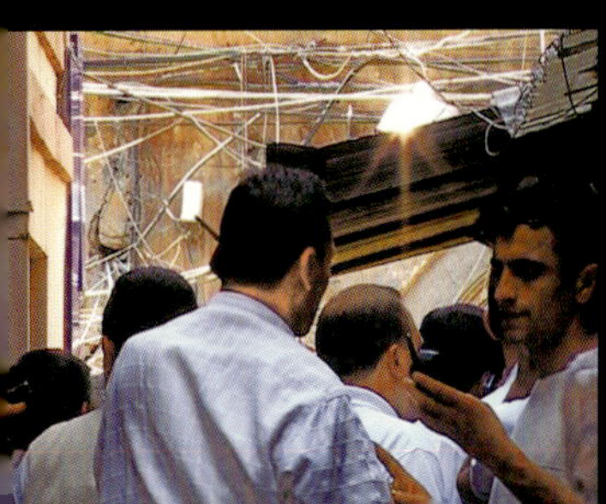

How much?
Don't be nasty. Can you send $50 000?
The dollar is flat, nothing happened.
It wouldn't go.
He is buying exact, exact.

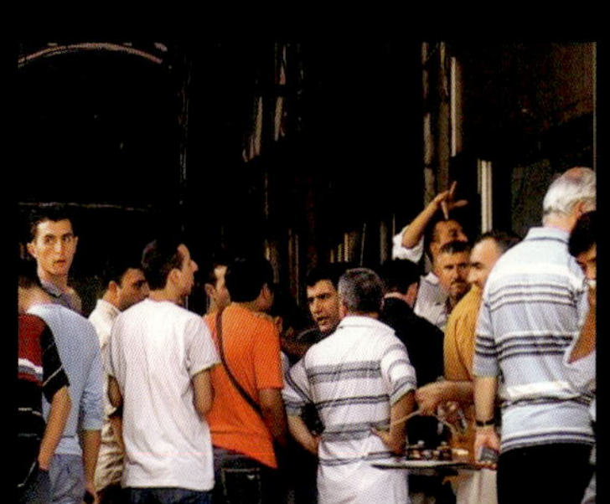

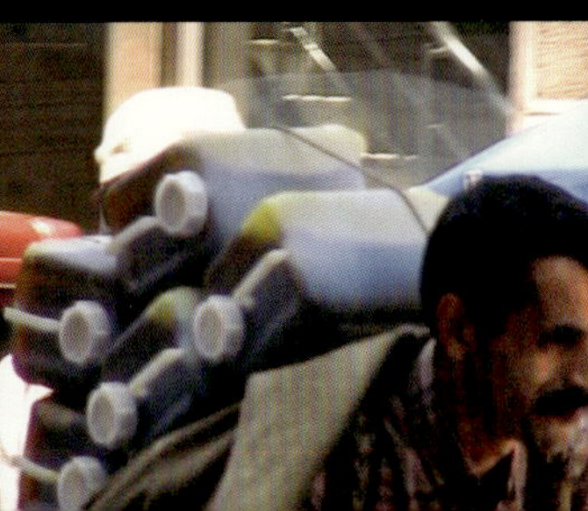

— Exact, I've got exact Euros.

— Cuneyt, Cuneyt, Cuneyt... send it ah.

— Hello, are you in the shop?

— 10 million — 15 million — what can you get?

— 100 million points.

— If it is two million, multiply the fucker.

— Zafer!

— It will be good to note this. There is definitely going to be a crisis for fuck's sake.

— Definitely a crisis...

— Don't tell me that nobody is interested; we've been going for two days.

— How much is it? Two billions?

— Half, half.

— What's happened boy?

— The banks started increasing it again, increasing it again.

— Doesn't he have a telephone?

— Exact Euros, 10,000 pieces exact Euros.

— How much?

— Don't be nasty. Can you send $50,000?

— The dollar is flat, nothing happened.

— It wouldn't go.

— He is buying exact, exact.

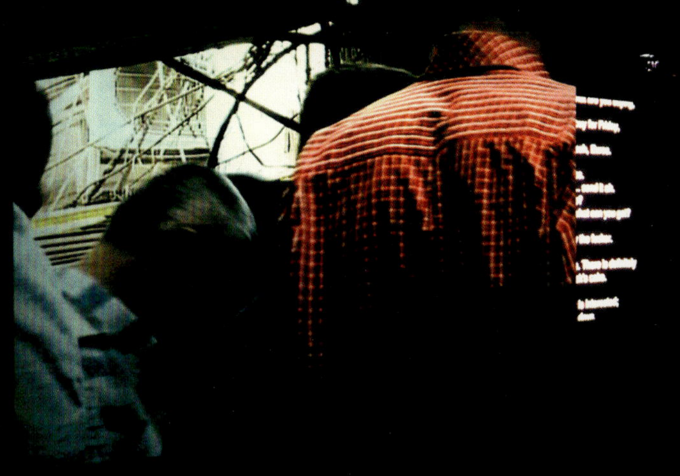

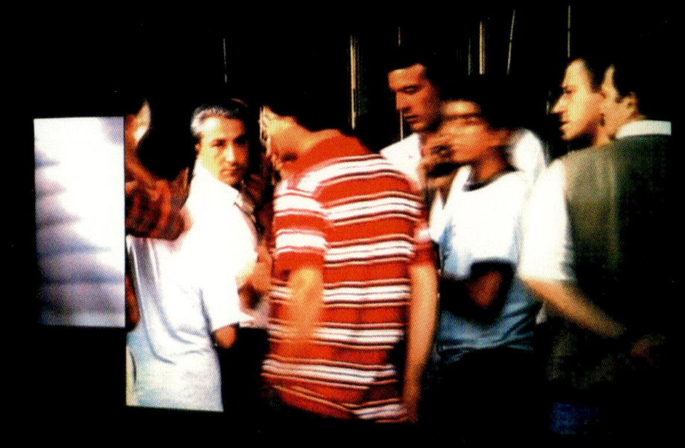

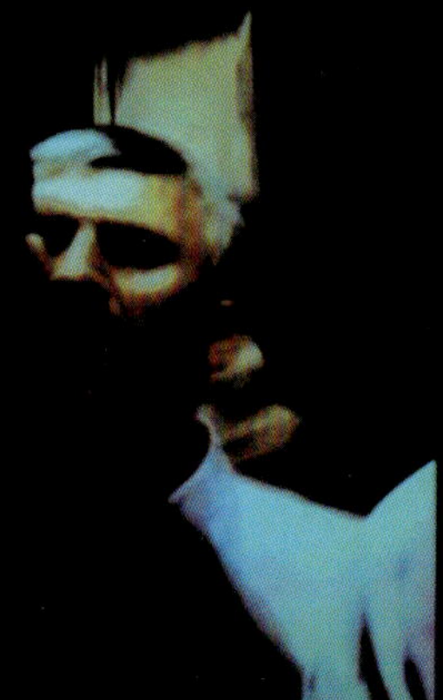

Hot, hot simit!
If the interest is two million per month,
fucking multiply it, 100 000.
It's necessary that the banks lend it. And if
the interest is 50%?
You wouldn't buy dollars this time.
Euros, is anybody selling Euros?
Gentlemen, I'm going. What are you saying,
it's ready?
Ahmet Bey, it's ready to buy for Friday,
for tomorrow.
I am buying Euros with cash, Euros.
With cash!
Exact, I've got exact Euros.
Cuneyt, Cuneyt, Cuneyt... send it ah.
Hello, are you in the shop?
10 million – 15 million – what can you get?

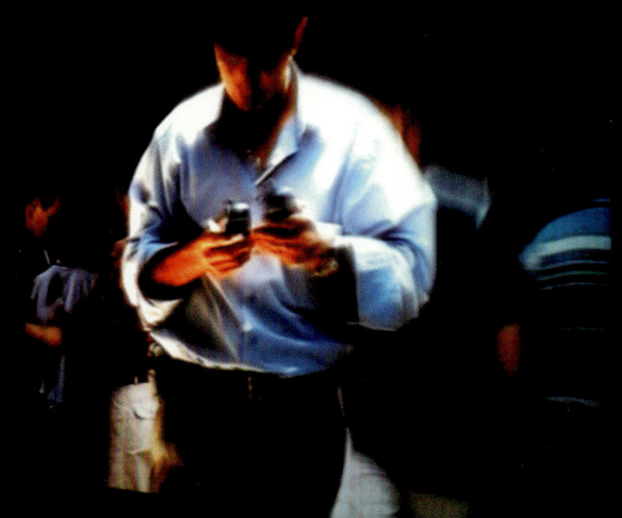

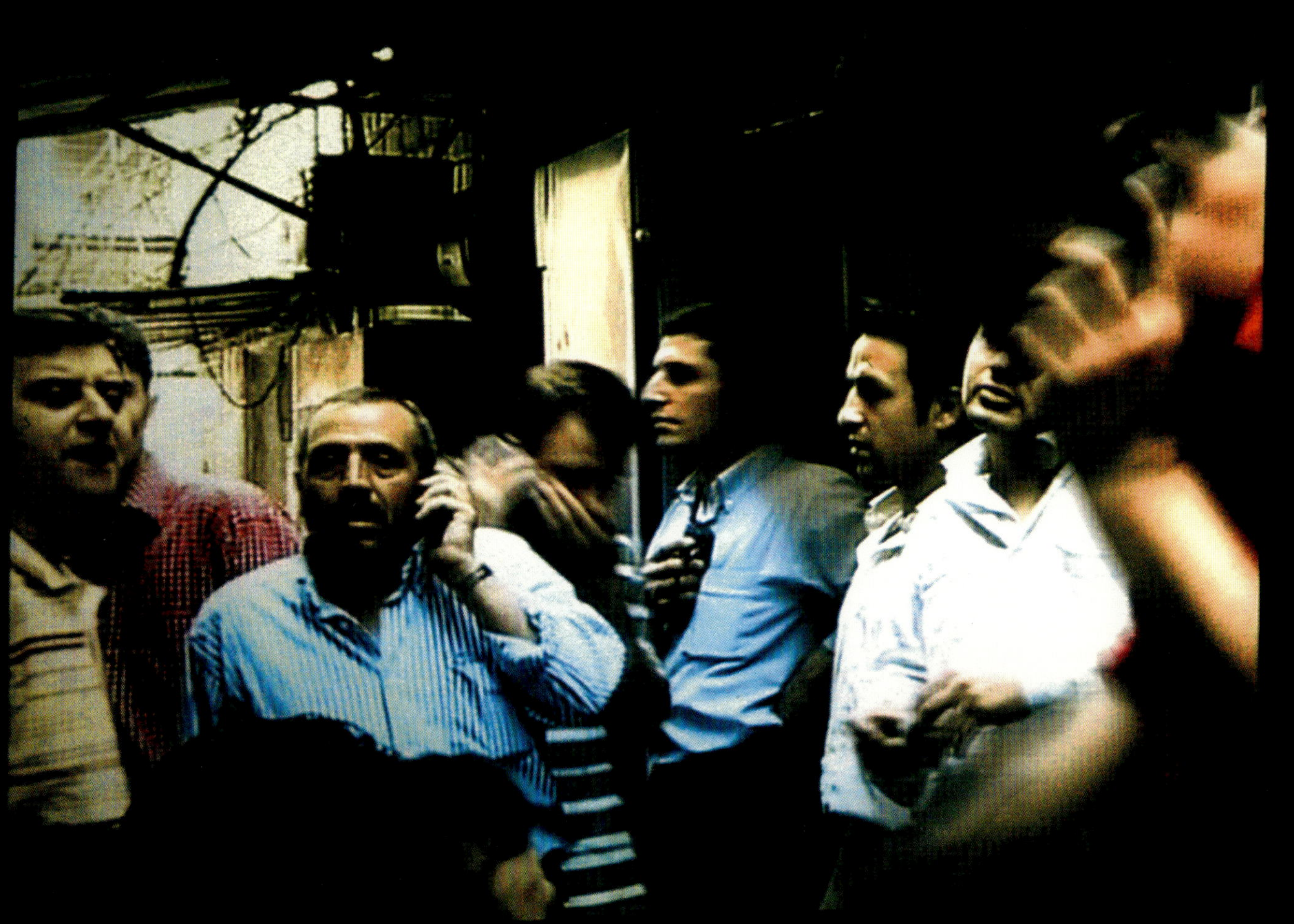

With ca
Exact, I
Cuneyt,
Hello, a
10 millio
100 mil
If it is to
Zafer!
It will be
going to
Definitel
Don't tel
we've be
How mu
Half, hal
What's h
The ban

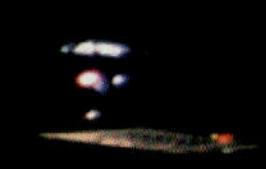
act Euros.
Cuneyt... send it ah.
he shop?
llion – what can you get?
multiply the fucker.
note this. There is definitely
is for fuck's sake.
nobody is interested;
for two days.
Two billions?
boy?
increasing it again,

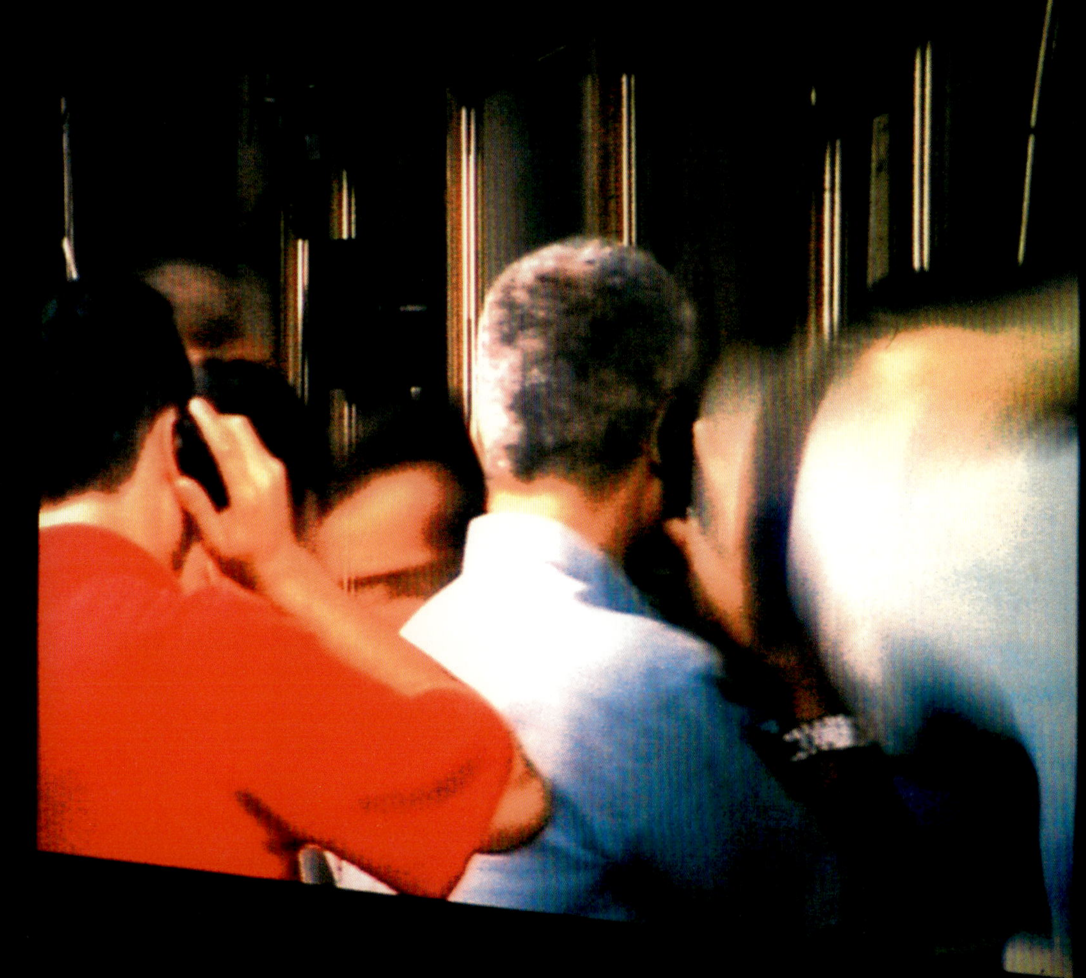

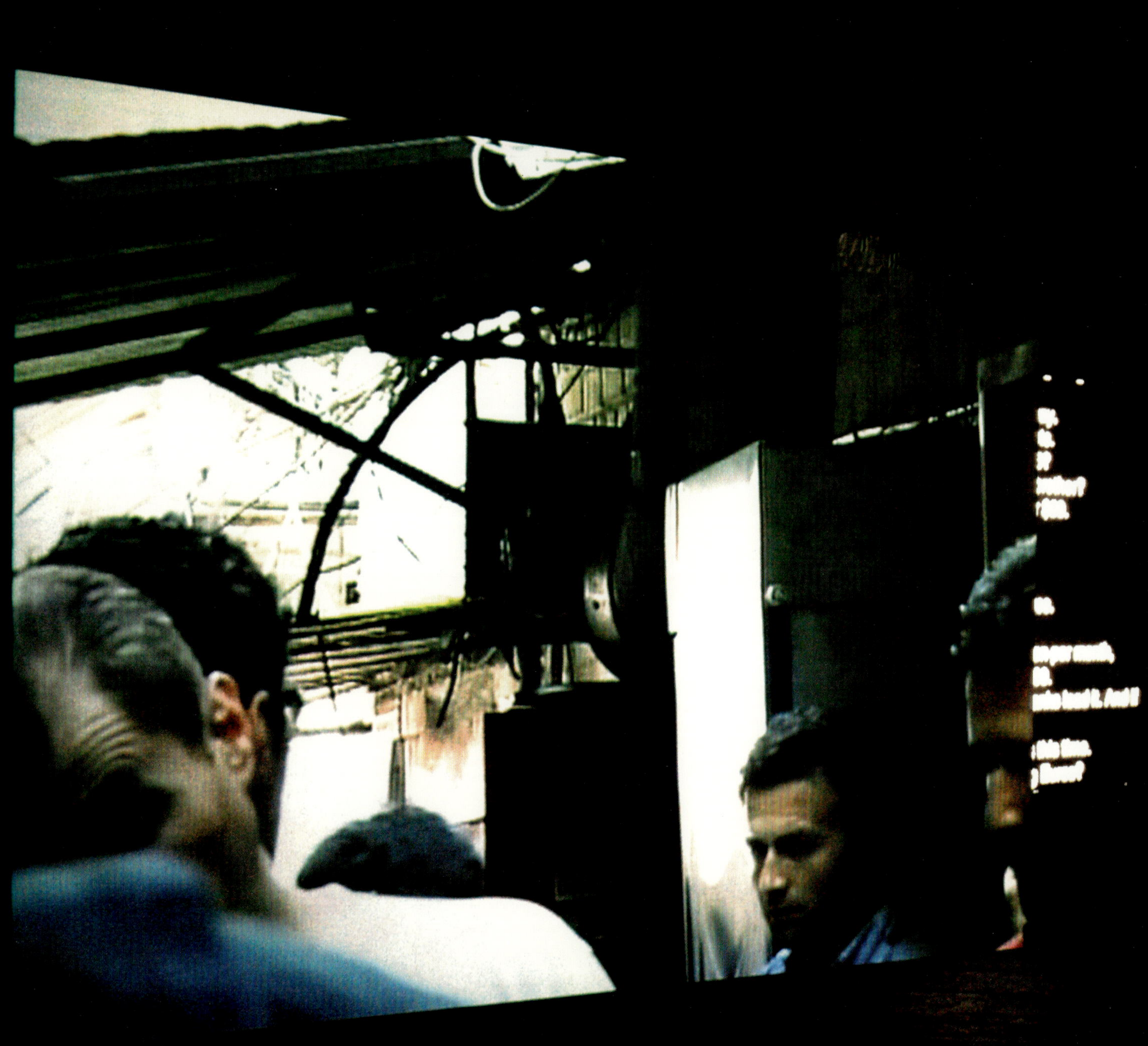

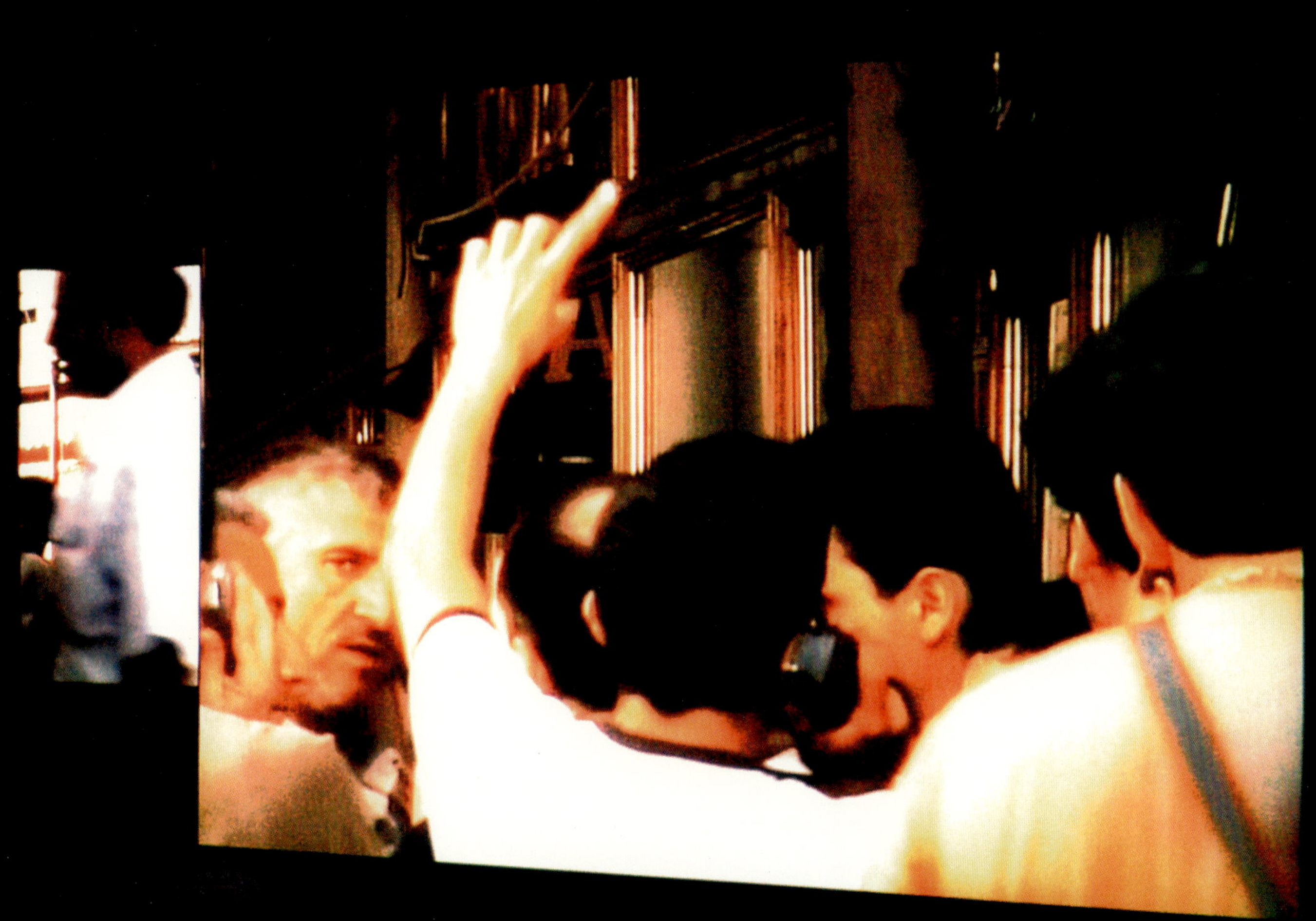

Buy for Monday.
Exact, I've got exact Euros.
Hot, hot simiiit!
If the interest is two million per month,
fucking multiply it, 100 000.
It's necessary that the banks load it. And if
the interest is 50%?
You wouldn't buy dollars this time.
Euros, is anybody selling Euros?
Gentlemen, I'm going. What are you saying,
it's ready?
Ahmet Bey, it's ready to buy for Friday,
for tomorrow.
I am buying Euros with cash, Euros.
With cash!
Exact, I've got exact Euros.
Cuneyt, Cuneyt, Cuneyt... send it ah.

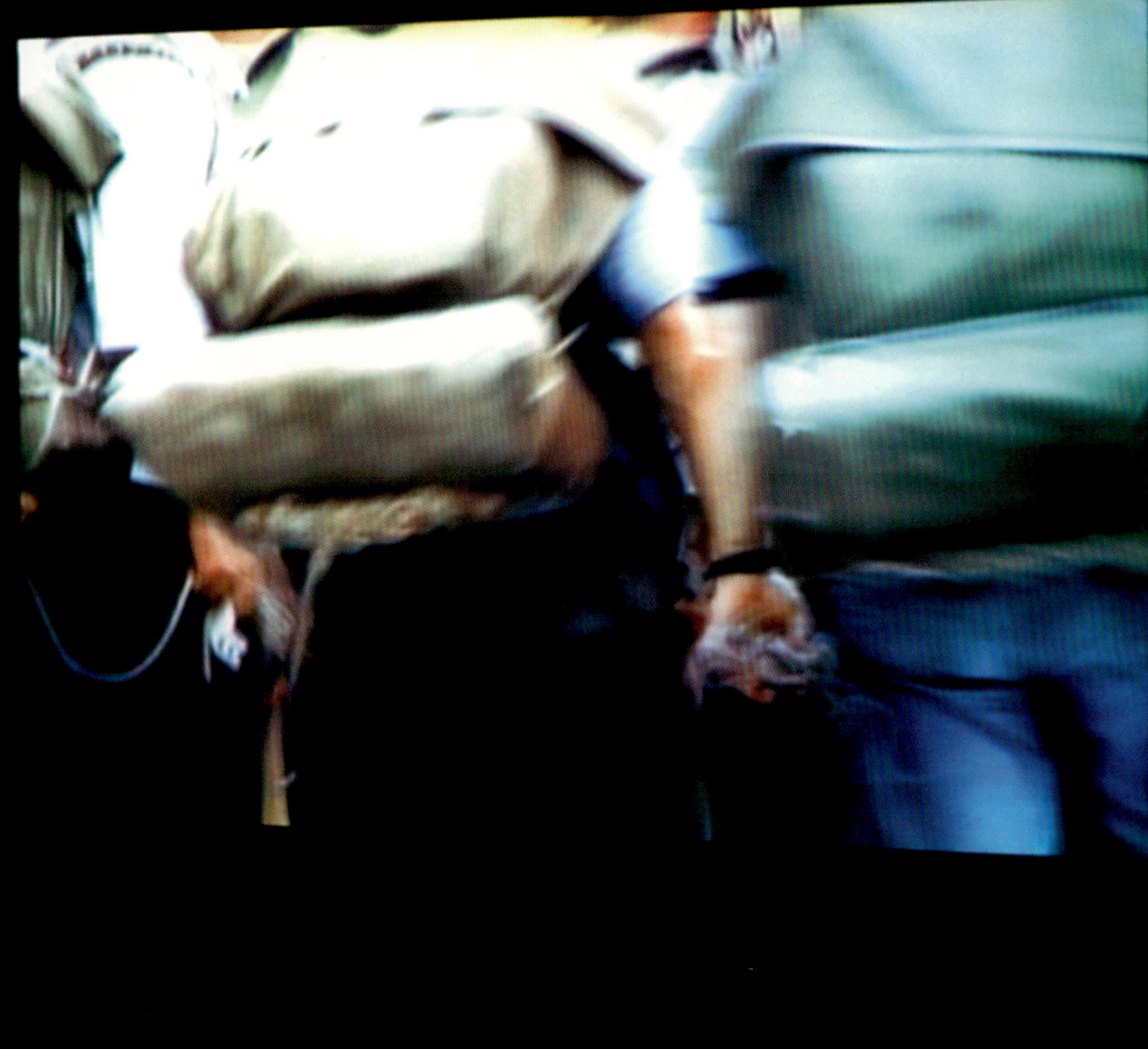

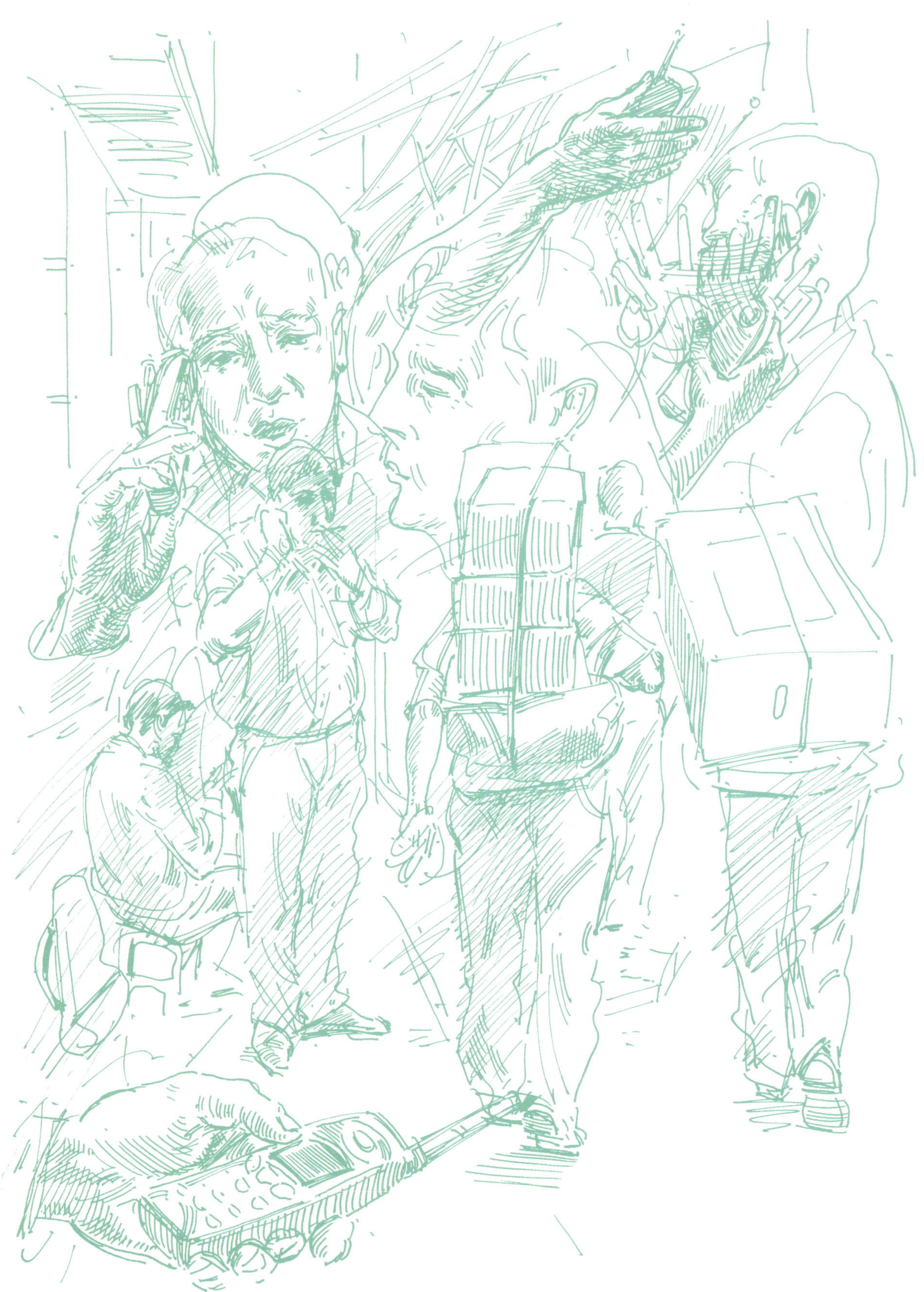

istanbul

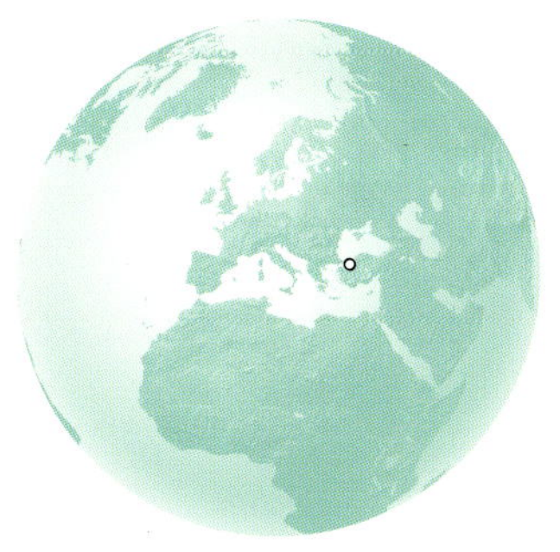

Itinerary

Istanbul (40° 58′N, 28° 50′E)–Grand Bazaar–Tahtakale Market–Central Bank of Turkey

Eastern and Western Approaches

Cruise ships moor up near to the Dolmabahçe Palace, not far from the 'Golden Horn', so named, legend has it, because the Byzantines had only time to ditch their wealth as Constantinople was overrun by invading Ottoman armies. Most modern ships pass this cornucopia silently in the night bound for the Black Sea with their dark cargoes, but for the tourist the Grand Bazaar is a must see.

Orientation and Sights

The Grand Bazaar

On the European side of the Bosphorus, behind Hagia Sofia, the Grand Bazaar is the world's largest covered oriental market with an expanse that encompasses 58 streets and 4000 shops. It was built in 1461 by Mehmet the Conqueror and has survived earthquake in 1896 and more recently fire in 1954 to retain its reputation as a treasure trove of eastern trade. It specialises in spices and carpets, embroideries and ceramics, gold and diamond jewellery, and there are even icons to be found in cave-like shops along the labyrinthine alleyways, strangely graced by magnificent arcades and cupolas. Many of the shops are grouped by kind of business practised: for instance the trade in spices has its own distinctive domain, Mısır Çarşısı. Nearby, Dõgbank is an emporium specialising in contraband electronic goods, *beyaz eşya*: quite literally 'white goods' but here in a black market setting. Another such artful clustering, still in the Grand Bazaar just north of Hasırcılar Caddesi and sitting atop a hill above the spice traders, is Tahtakale (in English a 'wooden fortress' or 'citadel'), a parallel currency market.

Mısır Çarşısı and Dõgbank

The spice market in Eminönu, Mısır Çarşısı, or Egyptian Spice Bazaar, dates from 1660 and is the place where locals come for traditional Turkish sweets, teas and unusual spices from Africa and the East that are unobtainable in other parts of Istanbul.

Not far from here, in Sirkeci, there is an Ottoman post office, the Büyük Postane, worth a look in itself, but also marking the spot where trucks unload hot goods from the Far East for the smugglers market. You can often see a line of porters, or *hamal*, carrying the merchandise in grey sacks up the hill to the market, Doğbank (which literally translates as 'eastern bank'), just as they have done for a century or more.

Tahtakale Currency Market

Tahtakale is hidden away in a tiny alley in Sirkeci not far from Hamam Çarşısı, near a gateway to the market, and is housed in a beautiful baroque arcade that is always a hive of activity. Open from 10:00–18:00, it remains one of the key, if obscure, institutions of Istanbul, a barometer of rates of exchange and economic trends that indirectly inform and influence national fiscal policy. On average some twenty five million dollars, or *tam* (meaning 'perfect'), are traded here everyday. If fortunes end up on the rocks beyond the Anatolian lighthouse at the downward straits of the Bosphorus, Tahtakale will probably have forecast it. As Turkey approaches EU membership this historic market will probably disappear.

Simon Harvey

Born 1968 in Targoviste, Bulgaria
Lives and works in London

Education

1994-95 MA Fine Art, Goldsmiths College, University of London
1990-94 BA Painting, University of Marmara, Istanbul
1982–87 I. Petrov School of Fine Arts, Sofia

Selected Solo Exhibitions

2006	Point of Departure, John Hansard Gallery, Southampton
	Point of Departure, Northern Gallery for Contemporary Art, Sunderland
2004	Poised in the Infinite Ocean & Tahtakale, Haunch of Venison, London
	Entanglement, Dundee Contemporary Arts, Dundee
2002	Resonance, Galerist, Istanbul
2001	Bildbegehren, dontmiss, Frankfurt
2000	Vitrine, Transit Space, London
1998	New Works, Duncan Cargill Gallery, London
1997	Haunting Presence, Duncan Cargill Gallery, London
1996	BM Contemporary Art Centre, Istanbul

Selected Group Exhibitions

2006	British Art Show 6, Arnolfini, Bristol*
	British Art Show 6, Nottingham Castle, Nottingham*
	Forest Man, The New Gallery, Jerusalem*
	Strangers With Angelic Faces, Akbank Art Centre, Istanbul*
	British Art Show 6, Manchester Art Gallery, Manchester*
2005	Something of the Night 1875–2005, Leeds City Art Gallery, Leeds
	Video London, Espai Ubú, Barcelona
	Radiance: Glasgow Festival of Light, Merchant City, Glasgow
	British Art Show 6, BALTIC, Gateshead*
	Der Knochen der Zunge, Kunstverein Medienturm, Graz
	Contaging with Nature, Akbank Art Centre, Istanbul
	On Patrol, De Appel Centre for Contemporary Art, Amsterdam
2004	Perspective, Ormeau Baths Gallery, Belfast*
	The Progressive Development Plan, The Empire, London*
	Whitstable Biennale 2004, Kent*
	Britannia Works, organised by The British Council, Xippas Gallery, Athens*
	3rd Berlin Biennial for Contemporary Art*
	Beck's Futures 2004, ICA, London; CCA, Glasgow*
2003	Poetic Justice, 8th International Istanbul Biennial, Istanbul*
	La Biennale di Venezia 50th International Art Exhibition*
2002	Look Again, Proje4L Istanbul Museum of Contemporary Art
	FAIR, Royal College of Art Galleries, London*
2001	Look Away, Platform Gallery, ARCO Madrid
1999	Medway Open, Royal Engineers' Museum Gallery, Gillingham*
1998	Roundtrip, Borusan Culture and Art Centre, Istanbul*
	Minus, Duncan Cargill Gallery, London
1996	Future Vision, The Photographers' Gallery, London

* denotes exhibition catalogue

Selected Publications

2005 Display, Edited by Pablo Lafuente, Rachmaninoff's, London
Neighbours in Dialogue, Nermin Saybasili, Norgunk, Istanbul
2004 Britannia Works, British Council, Athens
2002 Istanbul Pedestrian Exhibitions I: Nişantaşi — Personal Geographies, Global Maps, Kolektif Produksiyon, Istanbul
60 Years 60 Artists, Eczacibasi Virtual Museum, Istanbul

Selected Exhibition Reviews

2006 Robert Clark, The Guide, The Guardian (18th February)
Andrew Hunt, Frieze (January–February)
Neil Mulholland, British Art Show 6, Flash Art (January–February)
2005 Stuart Comer, London, Artforum (December)
David Briers, Something of the Night, Art Monthly (December–January)
British Art Show, Sunday Herald (2nd October)
Adrian Searle, State of the art, The Guardian (27th September)
Arifa Akbar, As Hirst hits 40, meet new faces of UK art scene, The Independent (6th June)
Steven Bode, Not Fade Away..., Contemporary (Issue 71)
Maureen Freely, Times Online (21st March)
Der Knochen der Zunge, Salzburger Nachrichten (17th March)
Kutluğ Ataman, The Daily Telegraph (18th December)
Craig Burnett, The Guide, The Guardian (23rd October)
2004 Peter Chapman, Nahum Tevet & Ergin Çavuşoğlu, The Independent (11th Sept 2004)
Catriona Black, Outer Limits, Sunday Herald (19th September)
Sophia Phoca, Britannia Works, Contemporary (Issue 65)
Moira Jeffrey, It's all in the mind, The Herald (3rd September)
Was Will Europa?, Flash Art (July–September)
Martin Coomer, Time Out London (7th April)
Richard Cork, Surveillance culture, New Statesman (12th April)
Adrian Searle, Full steam ahead, The Guardian (30th March)
Waldemar Januszczak, The Sunday Times, Culture (28th March)
Art Review (April)
Art Monthly (April)
Sleaze (April)
Rod Liddle, Tosh and Beck's, The Times (27th March)
Moira Jeffrey, Space is the artistic frontier, The Herald (26th March)
The Guardian (24th March)
Thomas W. Eller, Berlin in Winter, Artnet (20th February)
St. Galler Tagblatt (19th February)
Maerkische Allgemeine (14th February)
Artforum (January)
2003 Art in America (December)
The Guardian (16th December)
The Times (16th December)
The Independent (16th December)
Evening Standard (16th December)
Time Out London, No. 1736 (26th November)
XXI journal of architectural culture (October)
Whose Justice? Reflections on the Istanbul Biennial 2003, Robert C. Morgan, NY Arts Magazine (October)
ART das Kunstmagazin (June)
Resonance at Galerist, Arredamento Mimarlik (June)
2002 Time Out Istanbul (April)
Time Out London, No. 1462 (26th August)

Selected Interviews

2006 Point of Departure, John Hansard Gallery, Southampton (May)
2005 British Art Show 6, Hayward Gallery – BALTIC, DVD
Tim Marlow, British Art Show 6, Channel 5 (11th October)
2004 Beck's Futures 2004, BBC4 (April)
2003 BBC1 London News (16th December)
My London: The Artist, BBCi News and BBCi London News (September)
1998 Who are your art parents?, Whitechapel Art Gallery, London (March)

Ergin Çavuşoğlu
Places of Departure

Published by Film and Video Umbrella and Haunch of Venison

Edited by Steven Bode
Editorial Assistance from Nina Ernst

Designed by SMITH
Victoria Forrest

Printed by EBS, Italy

All illustrations and photography by Ergin Çavuşoğlu

Publication supported by Arts Council England
With additional support from the University of Portsmouth

ISBN 190427022 0

Film and Video Umbrella
52 Bermondsey Street
London SE1 3UD
United Kingdom
T 020 7407 7755
F 020 7407 7766
E info@fvu.co.uk
W www.fvumbrella.com

Haunch of Venison
London
6, Haunch of Venison Yard
off Brook Street
London W1K 5ES
United Kingdom
T +44 (0) 20 7495 5050
F +44 (0) 20 7495 4050
london@haunchofvenison.com

Haunch of Venison
Zürich
Lessingstrasse 5
8002 Zürich
Switzerland
T +41 (0) 43 422 8888
F +41 (0) 43 422 8889
zurich@haunchofvenison.com

www.haunchofvenison.com

Contributors
Steven Bode is Director of Film and Video Umbrella.

Chris Darke is a writer and film critic based in London. His books include *Light Readings: Film Criticism and Screen Arts* (Wallflower Press) and a critical monograph on J-L Godard's *Alphaville* (I.B. Tauris).

Claire Doherty is Senior Research Fellow at the University of the West of England, Bristol where she leads Situations, a research and commissioning programme which investigates the significance of place and context in contemporary art. www.situations.org.uk

Simon Harvey lectures at the Art Academy of the University of Trondheim, Norway. He has written extensively on contemporary art, travel and cultural theory.

Ergin Çavuşoğlu would like to thank: Steven Bode, Matt Watkins, Tim Putnam, Chris Darke, Claire Doherty, Simon Harvey, Stuart Smith and Victoria Forrest for making this book possible. I am also grateful to the University of Portsmouth, to the Arts and Humanities Research Council and, of course, Haunch of Venison for supporting this publication and my work in general. Special thanks go to Bevis Bowden, Nina Ernst, Mike Jones, Caroline Smith, Jeremy Millar, Denizhan Özer, Taylan Halıcı, Alistair Robinson, Dean Turnbull, Stephen Foster, Ros Carter and Pernilla Holmes for the production and exhibition of *Point of Departure*. Finally, I would like to thank Katharina and our daughter Ella to whom I dedicate this book.

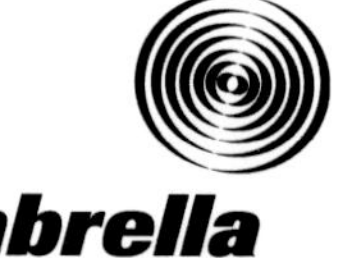

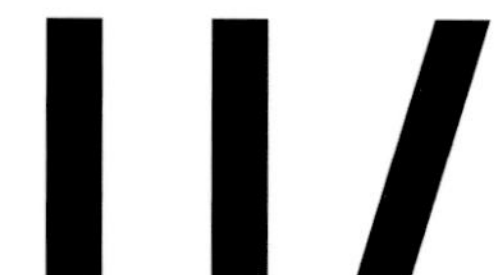

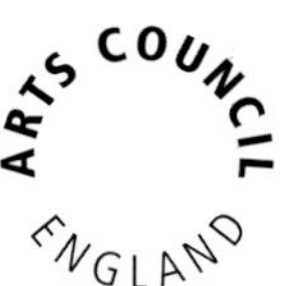